CASES IN

Direct
Marketing

SECOND EDITION

Herbert E. Brown

Paula M. Saunders

Bruce Buskirk

Foreword by Bob Stone

Printed on recyclable paper

NTC Business Books

a division of *NTC Publishing Group* • Lincolnwood, Illinois USA

Published by NTC Business Books, a division of NTC Publishing Group
4255 West Touhy Avenue
Lincolnwood (Chicago), Illinois 60646-1975, U.S.A.

5 6 7 8 9 ML 0 9 8 7 6 5 4 3 2 1

Contents

Part VI International Direct Marketing Cases

Foreword

I am one of a privileged few who has seen the steady and sometimes phenomenal growth of direct marketing over a period of five decades.

During this span, I have participated in this growth both as a practitioner and as an academic. Over the decades I have seen commonalities emerge between practitioners and academics. The case study method for solving marketing problems, long a purview of colleges and universities, is being embraced more and more by practitioners.

In their book, *Cases in Direct Marketing*, Professors Herbert Brown, Paula Saunders, and Bruce Buskirk take a giant step forward in making practitioners comfortable with the case study method for solving marketing problems. The authors provide the framework by exploring the five main elements in a well-developed case analysis.

The 23 real-life cases in this book provide practical examples for the practitioner of how the case study approach often leads to dynamic marketing solutions. The case study approach is likewise effective as a learning tool for marketing students.

So I commend *Cases in Direct Markeing* to you. It's a "good read," but more importantly, it's the book to reach for when you have a problem to solve!

Bob Stone, Chairman Emeritus
Stone & Adler, Inc.

Preface

Cases in Direct Marketing is comprised of actual direct marketing problems and situations, and therefore will benefit both beginning students of the field in their endeavor to learn direct marketing concepts and techniques, and more seasoned professionals who want to challenge and extend their mastery of direct marketing. Thus, this book is written for use in both colleges and professional settings.

Direct marketing is being utilized, in one of its many forms, in virtually every type of business or organization. Bachelor's and master's degrees in direct marketing are currently offered at several universities. One or more direct marketing courses are offered at hundreds more. Theoretical perspectives on direct marketing are now being advanced and researched by scholars. Direct marketing journals have been established as outlets for scholarly research, and trade journals have become numerous. Direct marketing trade books are increasingly in evidence, as are textbooks for use in collegiate teaching.

Direct marketing literature, as it must, emphasizes principles, concepts, definitions, and "what works" material. This information is, of course, immensely valuable to the aspiring professional. At some point, however, a practice context should be provided for the study of direct marketing. One of the best ways to provide this is with cases representing the diversity of direct marketing applications and problems. Accordingly, this book challenges the student with a variety of print and telemarketing cases and problems—some large and some small, some rich in data and some data poor—but all reflecting the reality of the direct marketing channel and industry.

Cases in this book offer educators opportunities to challenge and educate students in the creative thinking and problem-solving aspects of direct marketing at both the strategic and the tactical level. Some of the cases in this volume offer users opportunities to critique and learn from failures; others challenge the student or business user to improve on already successful direct marketing operations. Still others require original analysis and creative planning. Some involve the classic package, others the self-mailer, and still others the problems and opportunities of catalog marketing. Both consumer and business-to-business cases are included, as are cases ranging from lead generation and qualfication to go-for-the-order programs. Retail database, international, and direct marketing ethics cases are also represented in this edition.

Although this book focuses on perspectives and technologies that are distinctly direct marketing, it does not overlook the interrelationships of direct marketing with the general marketing field. The cases selected for inclusion in this book challenge the reader to reflect on the blending and melding of direct and general marketing.

We hope you find the material useful. Please let us know what you think and how it can be improved.

Good luck in your teaching and practice of direct marketing.

Herbert E. Brown and Paula M. Saunders

Introduction

Guidelines for Direct Marketing Case Analysis

Although they may vary in length, scope, and degree of difficulty, direct marketing cases usually have several things in common and, therefore, can be approached using the same general analytical framework. Normally, because the key to successful direct marketing is getting the "big things," the list, offer, positioning, format, and program structure, as close to right as possible, these will usually be prominent issues for analysis and resolution in all of the cases in this book.

Guidelines for Direct Marketing Case Presentation

Cases may be prepared and/or presented by individuals or by groups of peers, in both written and verbal forms. The prime criteria for evaluation of case presentations, in whichever mode, are the quality of the analysis and the communicative power of the presenter(s).

Written Presentations

Written presentations may be fully written out or in full outline form. Five main elements to a well-developed case analysis are as follows:

1. Identification and specification of the problem or objective.
2. Appraisal of the facts and opinions expressed in the case.
3. Development of alternative approaches to the case problem.
4. Selection and justification of the best approach.
5. Discussion of the implementation schedule and organizational responsibilities.

Evaluation of the presentation will consider the following dimensions:

- *Appearance, grammar, organization, and form.* Such items as clarity of expression, sentence and paragraph structure, and readability will be judged.

- *Problem definition, objective setting, and fact identification.* Such items as
  ability to distinguish between problems and symptoms, between
  sub-area and program objectives, and between fact and opinion
  will be assessed.
- *Alternative selection and evaluation.* Such elements as completeness,
  substantiation, and creativity of alternative identification and selection will be reviewed. The skill used in critiquing each alternative will be judged.
- *Selection and implementation.* Such items as the precision of strategy
  statement and the completeness of implementation considerations
  will be evaluated. Weakness in this area is as harmful as weakness in
  the problem/objective definition areas.

Oral Presentations

Oral presentations are often difficult for students but are an important aspect of the learning process. Portraying your ideas persuasive-
ly but tactfully is a delicate process, the mastery of which can only
be obtained through practice.

The oral presentations required will generally be in conjunction
with written case work. Evaluation of oral presentations will normally reflect the quality of work in each of the following:

1. Organization of presentation
2. Content (quality and thoroughness)
3. Quality of visual aids (visual aids are strongly recommended)
4. Speaking voice (delivery)
5. Courtesy to audience
6. Ability to answer questions
7. Posture, poise
8. Ability to defend position
9. Persuasive impact
10. Mannerisms
11. Practicality of recommendations

Case presentations are strengthened when presenters are aware of
and stop using undesirable mannerisms. Eight of the most common
and distracting of these follow[1]:

- *The Pray-er:* Presenter folds hands in front of body and looks as
  though he or she is praying to just make it through the presentation.

---

[1]Source: Adapted from *Personal Selling Power,* July/August 1984, pp. 8–9. Reprinted by
permission of Bryan Flanagan of the Zig Ziglar Corporation and author of the "Effective Business Presentations" seminar.

- *The Key Executive:* Presenter fiddles with keys, coins, and other wonderful things found in pockets.
- *The Jeweler:* Presenter plays with ring, watch, etc.
- *The Stern Parent:* Presenter stands with arms crossed over chest.
- *The Fig Leaf:* Presenter stands with hands folded in front, much as Adam must have looked in his first outfit.
- *The Soldier at Parade Rest:* Presenter holds hands behind back.
- *Dishpan Hands:* Presenter conceals hands in pockets so no one can see them.
- *The Athletic Type:* Presenter demonstrates athletic prowess with a running series of jabs, punches, upper cuts, karate chops, etc.

Group Presentations

Group work can be a vital part of a management preparatory course; therefore, students are often placed into working groups for completion of the assigned group cases. Individual roles, leadership functions, and the division of labor are usually left up to the individual groups. Each student is, however, normally expected to make a visible contribution to each group project.

There are many problems and frustrations associated with group work. These problems, however, are not exclusive to students. They extend far into the "real" business world, where one must contend with comparable "real" problems daily. Group presentations can provide the participants with invaluable experience in dealing with such problems.

Test Your Direct Marketing I.Q.[2]

Every direct marketing problem has its own unique characteristics and, therefore, a unique solution or set of solutions. However, there are some techniques and ideas that work in a large variety of direct marketing situations and contexts and are worth reviewing before attempting to solve any direct marketing problem. Some people refer to these and similar notions as the "rules" of direct marketing. They are the "rules" because they have been found to work more often than not. These are especially useful when you cannot test but have to roll out a program anyway, or when you are preparing a test. In either case, you want to maximize your chances of success. Practicing direct marketers use these rules and dozens of others. How well do you know them? Find out by identifying which of the following 36 statements are true and which are false and trying to explain why.

---

[2]Author's note: We have been unable to locate the original source of this material. If any reader can provide us with this information, we shall be delighted to acknowledge our indebtedness.

Mailing Format

_____ 1. The most effective mailing package consists of an outside envelope, letter, circular, response form, and business reply envelope or card.
_____ 2. The circular or brochure ranks first in importance.

Letters

_____ 3. Form letters using indented paragraphs usually outpull those in which indented paragraphs are not used.
_____ 4. Underlining pertinent phrases and sentences usually increases results slightly.
_____ 5. A combined letter and circular will generally do better than a separate letter and separate circular in the same package.
_____ 6. It is best to disclose the price and payment terms early in a sales letter.
_____ 7. A form letter with a display headline will ordinarily do better than a filled-in, personalized letter.
_____ 8. Authentic testimonials in a sales letter ordinarily increase the pull.
_____ 9. A one-page letter ordinarily outpulls a two-page letter.
_____ 10. Computer letters always outpull printed letters.

Brochures

_____ 11. A brochure that deals specifically with the proposition presented in the letter will be more effective than a brochure of an institutional nature.
_____ 12. Employing all art or all photography in a circular will usually result in a better brochure than one employing a combination of art and photography.
_____ 13. Deluxe, large-size, color brochures almost always prove cost-efficient in the sale of big-ticket products.

Outside Envelopes

_____ 14. Illustrated envelopes always detract from a mailing's effectiveness.
_____ 15. In a series of mailings, it is important to standardize the type and size of the outside envelope.

Order Forms

_____ 16. Reply cards with receipt stubs will usually increase response over cards with no stubs.

_____ 17. Adding a toll-free "800" response telephone number to the order form will increase response.

Reply Cards or Envelopes

_____ 18. Postage-free business reply cards or envelopes will generally bring in no more responses than those to which the respondent must affix postage.

_____ 19. An airmail reply envelope usually increases responses to impulse offers.

Color

_____ 20. One-color letters usually pull as well or better than two-color letters.

_____ 21. A two-color brochure generally proves more effective than a one-color brochure.

_____ 22. Full color brochures are almost always cost-effective, regardless of offer.

Postage

_____ 23. Third class mail ordinarily pulls as well as first class mail.

_____ 24. In business-to-business mailing, bulk postage stamps usually pull better than metered postage.

General Information

_____ 25. Nothing is more important to the success of a mailing than good, sound creative.

_____ 26. In a two-step lead-generation offer, it's important to involve the sales force to assure maximum success.

_____ 27. In most cases for most products, mailing in July and August is just as good as mailing in January or September.

The Offer

_____ 28. Before a catalog is started, the theme is the most important element.

_____ 29. You should look at a direct-response television ad more as an audio and visual direct mail package than as a normal consumer television commercial with a phone number at the end.

_____ 30. The most effective direct-response television spots are usually 60 seconds or less.

_____ 31. The telephone can serve as a supplement or alternative to other direct-response media.

_____ 32. Anyone can make an unscripted telephone solicitation call.

_____ 33. Next to direct mail, newspapers are more widely used by direct marketers than any other medium.

_____ 34. Bind-in magazine insert cards usually are cost-efficient.

_____ 35. Direct-response newspaper ads tend to produce orders nearly as quickly as television advertising.

_____ 36. Co-op mailings, card decks, and package inserts are relatively expensive direct-response media.

Timeless Direct Marketing Principles

In addition to the rules mentioned in the preceding section, the rich history of direct marketing has also produced what have been called Timeless Direct Marketing Principles[3] by Bob Stone. The 21 principles listed below include some of Stone's principles (in modified form) and others selected by the authors.

1. You have to hunt for the productive part of any list. The Pareto Principle applies here; thus, give or take a few percentage points, you can count on 80 percent of your sales of goods and services coming from 20 percent, or less, of an acquired list, or from 20 percent, or less, of your customer base.

2. It is not the first order—the sale, but the second order that is critical to direct marketing success. Money is often lost on the first sale to a buyer. The second and subsequent sales can be very profitable because they often cost less than half as much as the first sale. That is why customer satisfaction is so important. The order is 1) make a sale to a prospect, 2) get a repeat purchase from a first-time buyer, and then 3) convert the repeat buyer to customer.

---

[3]Bob Stone, *Successful Direct Marketing Methods*, NTC, 1994, pp. 5+.

3. Carefully crafted offers must be creatively and effectively positioned to the right lists if direct marketing success is to be maximized. All three basic direct marketing strategy elements—list, offer, and positioning—are critical.

4. If your program cannot sell those prospects who need your offer the most, and are therefore the easiest to sell, it is not likely to be successful with more marginal prospects or customers. Therefore, test with your best customers and/or prospects, and even test during the best time of the year; then, if successful, roll out to the rest.

5. Prospects whose names appear on two or more direct-response lists (multibuyers who have bought more often and/or a greater variety by direct response) will respond better to your offer than will prospects who have bought from only one list. These people are likely to be "direct response responsives." They are the lifeblood of most direct mail businesses.

6. Lists containing only names of people who are known to have purchased from a direct response channel are more likely to be profitable than lists of names that have been compiled for some other reason (for example, they have purchased clothing at a retail store similar to what you market by mail order).

7. The more characteristics you can infer about names on a list, or predict that a name on a list might have (home ownership, marital status), the more likely you are to sell effectively to that list. That is why overlays on lists (determined, for example, by the zip code location of the name), sometimes called list enhancements, such as income, marital status, and life-style characteristics, often pay big dividends.

8. Remailing (within a reasonable time) a list that pulled successfully is usually a good idea; from 40 to 60 percent of the first mailing response is often obtained from follow-up mailings to the same list within 30 days.

9. Leaving no doubt about the action you want improves response. Direct marketers even find that "Yes/No" offers consistently pull better than merely asking for a "Yes." Asking prospects for action is what distinguishes direct-response advertising from image advertising.

10. Direct-mail response rate and average order will be higher when prospects can pay by credit card—in most cases about twice as high. Payment method is part of the offer. Any change in an offer can make a big difference in response rates. Beware of how you slice it, though. For example, long term, half as much response from a cash-with-order offer may translate into higher

profits later because the cash-with-order requirement generated a higher-quality customer.

11. Specificity sells. For example, limiting offers to specific dates generates more responses than no-time-limit offers. Using concrete, clear copy also increases returns. Telling prospects exactly what they are going to get is the direct marketing pathway both to higher customer satisfaction and higher profits. Likewise, fundraisers get far more money when they ask for a specific amount and tie the contribution to a specific project. Fast talk and small print have no place in legitimate direct marketing. We want to satisfy customers, not swindle them. Be clear.

12. Sweepstakes work. Overlaying direct marketing offers (especially consumer impulse item offers) with sweepstakes typically improves response rates by a third or more. Sweeps also work in business-to-business direct marketing.

13. Throwing in a free gift does more for response rates than does lowering price. Usually, one can more creatively merchandise a gift than a discount of comparable value. "Free Gift," in spite of the redundancy, works.

14. Endless description of product features will sell some products, but succinct and creative presentation of benefits will sell a lot more. Even then, the buyer has to have a problem before what a product can do for him or her becomes a benefit. Choosing which benefit to emphasize (which buyer problem to address) is what is happening when the offer is being positioned. Positioning is what your communication and creative does for the product in the mind of the buyer, not what you do to a product.

15. Long sales letters work if they are interesting and answer questions in the minds of buyers. A letter (in fact, copy in general) has to be long enough and complete enough to answer all of a buyer's questions. Unanswered questions mean non-response. The more you are asking the buyer to do—the bigger the commitment—the more questions you will have to answer. "Send cash" requires more answers than "Let us know you're interested by sending in the attached coupon." The sales letter is the hardest-working component of the classic direct response package—it works harder than the outside envelope, brochure or circular, lift device/premium, or order form or other response device.

16. Renewal of subscriptions to financial newsletters, magazines, and so on, and repurchase of products or services is due more to the product or service itself than clever direct-response copy or

the use of other direct marketing techniques. Marketing cannot overcome customer resistance caused by the fact that a product or service does not meet buyers' expectations or solve their problems.

17. Self-mailers, card decks, and the like cost less than most envelope-enclosed mailings, but they likewise almost always produce less response. The self-mailer is one of three basic direct-response formats. The others are the classic package and the catalog. Order-cost analysis and lifetime-value-of-the-customer analysis are mandatory to make sure that the most cost-effective direct response format is being used.

18. It is easier to increase a direct marketing program's average order size than it is to increase the program's response rate. It is also usually easier to up-sell (sell more of the same item) than it is to cross-sell (sell a related item).

19. Put your proven winners on the front of your catalog, and in the front pages, when you want more first-time buyers for your catalog. Also, make your catalog bigger (for example, go from 24 to 32 pages) if you want to sell more of your line—assuming the products are of similar appeal. Mailing your catalog to your current catalog customers will give maximum response—current customers usually respond from four to eight times as well as names on untested lists.

20. Using one medium to call buyer attention to an offer presented in another medium can dramatically increase response. For example, a television support commercial can increase response to a newspaper insert by 50 percent.

21. Make sure your direct-response ad has all of the four elements required to be a direct-response ad: a definite offer, enough information to make the decision being requested, a request for action, and content that is targeted to a definite list or list segment based on data about each name or list of names selected to receive the ad.

Direct Marketing Cases for Consumer Products and Services

Cases in this section illustrate the conceptual and operational direct marketing underpinnings of consumer direct marketing programs while challenging the reader to understand the major direct marketing media, tools, principles, and skills that drive successful participation in the business-to-consumer direct marketing channel.

The section begins with *U.S. Auto* and *Bull Markets,* two powerful examples of direct marketing failures which challenge the reader to take a holistic view of direct marketing strategy while demonstrating the substantial knowledge and skill required to be successful in direct marketing. Strategic issues related to list, offer, positioning, and format, and the importance of finding the right combination of these, are explored in depth in several cases, particularly in *Baby Blankets by Mail* and *Allwood Chef, Inc.* The closely-related issues of media testing and assessing the pulling power of different creative or positioning messages for consumer direct marketing programs are the focus of the *Letters* and *Magna Deca* cases.

Channel conflict and the viability of selling a new product through the direct marketing channel are two problems common to direct business-to-consumer marketing. The conflict that is always potentially present when a firm uses a multi-channel marketing and distribution system is explored in *Workmate, Inc.,* a case that also reveals how challenging the resolution of channel conflict can be.

Assessing the viability of selling a new product through the direct marketing channel and designing the appropriate program for it are the concerns faced in *Select Communications, Inc.* and *PreFone Integrated Products, Inc. Dudes* is an especially interesting case since it involves the problems encountered when introducing an intangible service rather than a tangible good.

This introductory section also includes *Complete Petmart* and *Helzberg Diamond Shops, Inc.,* two cases which illustrate the growing strategic necessity and prominence of effective relationship-building using database marketing.

Case 1

U.S. Auto

Assessment of a Direct Marketing Failure

U.S. Auto was unaccustomed to failure, having had a long string of significant successes in various automotive after-market related businesses. So it was with great confidence that it set up a new company, U.S. Warranty, to sell yet another automotive product—road hazard insurance for automobile tires.

The market target selected for the initial sales effort was new car buyers who had chosen to have their cars rust-proofed through the auto dealer's rust-proofing program, rather than by Ziebart or by another major rust-proofing firm. U.S. Auto supplied these dealers with their rust-proofing program and materials. Guarantees of the rust-proofing by U.S. Auto led to its having access to all new car buyers who used its service. These names became the target market chosen by U.S. Auto.

An average weekly flow of 4,000 names of new-car buyers—which seemed to be an ideal list for a direct mail program—was available to U.S. Auto/U.S. Warranty. It was not strictly a "hotline" list (recent direct response buyers), of course, but it was timely, and everyone on it seemed to be a logical prospect for a road-hazard insurance offer. Not only was every name known to have the characteristic "new-car buyer," but the brand name of auto purchased and a host of other purchaser characteristics, such as zip code of residence, were also known.

U.S. Auto decided to test its road hazard insurance concept before rollout. An assortment of approaches were discussed, and the resulting test self-mailer (see Exhibit 1-1) was chosen on the basis of its simplicity and low cost. The in-the-mail cost of the piece was $14 per thousand. (The list was free!) The breakeven pull rate was one order per thousand or only a tenth of a percent.

U.S. Auto used the name "U.S. Warranty" for the very first time in the promotion. This was done to improve the fit of the company name and the product. A new address was also chosen so prospects could not identify the well-known U.S. Auto by its corporate address.

Executives were dumbfounded by the test results—one order for the entire test mailing of four thousand new car buyers. One executive felt that the sample mailing was too small to be reflective.

Exhibit 1-1   U.S. Auto's Test Self-Mailer

U.S. Warranty
P.O. Box 206
Millersport, Ohio 43046

IMPORTANT
NEW CAR
INFORMATION
INSIDE

U.S. Warranty
P.O. Box 206
Millersport, Ohio 43046

POSTAGE WILL BE PAID BY ADDRESSEE

FIRST CLASS   PERMIT NO. 8   MILLERSPORT, OHIO 43046

BUSINESS REPLY CARD

NO POSTAGE
NECESSARY
IF MAILED
IN THE
UNITED STATES

Exhibit 1-1   U.S. Auto's Test Self-Mailer

ARE YOU AWARE THAT THE TIRES ON YOUR NEW CAR DO NOT HAVE A WARRANTY?

Major tire companies no longer provide you with a road hazard guarantee on tires. We do! For the first 24 months or 24,000 miles, you won't have to spend another dime on those tires. We will repair any flat tire you get... and we'll replace any nonrepairable tire, whatever the reason. No hassle. No excuses. No questions. Even more, for the next 12 months, we will replace your tire on a pro rata basis.

Here's how your U.S. Warranty protects your tires:

• **FLAT TIRE REPAIR**—Reimburses you for the reasonable cost of repairing any flat tire in connection with a warranty claim. This repair can be made by any tire servicing facility that is convenient for you.

• **ROAD HAZARD**—If your tire is damaged by a road hazard and cannot be repaired:

  You will receive reimbursement for the reasonable cost for a comparable new tire for the first 24 months or 24,000 miles, whichever occurs first.

  For the next 12 months or 12,000 miles, whichever occurs first, you will be reimbursed for the pro rata portion of the reasonable cost of a comparable replacement tire.

Yes!

I want to take advantage of U.S. Warranty's Introductory Offer and protect my tires against road hazards for only $29.95.

MasterCard · VISA

Your warranty, backed by one of the oldest firms issuing extended automobile warranties, will be sent to you in 2 to 4 weeks. If you are not completely satisfied, your money will be refunded within 30 days.

Name _____

Address_____

City _____

State _____ Zip _____

Order your U.S. Warranty tire protection by completing this order form and mailing today! Enclose your check or money order in an envelope and send to the address on the reverse side, or, use this convenient postage paid order form with your MasterCard or Visa Charge.

☐ Enclosed is my personal check for $29.95 payable to U.S. Warranty.

☐ Please charge my _____ MasterCard _____ Visa $29.95.

Card No. _____

Interbank No. _____

Expiration Date _____

Signature _____

Questions

1. Critique the self-mailer shown in Exhibit 1-1 for conformance to what is known to work in direct-response marketing. Was the mailing a valid test of the concept? What could the company have done to improve the test before rerunning it?
2. Do you think the concept offers enough promise to revise the program and retest?
3. What are the positive and negative aspects of the list selected by U.S. Auto?
4. Is the offer a particularly strong one?
5. Is the copy consistent with good direct-response copy?

Case 2

Bull Markets
Selling Vitamins with Print Advertising

Al Binkley thought he had a great idea. It involved direct-response marketing of vitamins—more specifically, a vitamin designed especially for the financial community—using direct-response newspaper ads. The product was a multivitamin similar in content to such well-known brands as One-A-Day and StressTabs. He called his brand "Bull Markets."

The product's label described it as "a high-potency, multimineral formula containing 25 essential daily vitamins and minerals—with no preservatives, starch, or sugar added." Each bottle contained 30 tablets. Al purchased his vitamin supply with his "Bull Market" label on the bottle from a repackager.

Al planned to sell the product for $5 per bottle. He estimated his in-the-mail fulfillment costs to be $2 per bottle, so he had a $3-per-bottle profit contribution margin to pay for his promotion costs. Thus, his first effort at selling the product, which cost him $800 to design and place in the paper, had a 267-bottle break-even requirement. Al's first effort was an ad in the financial section of a Sunday edition of the Columbus, Ohio *Dispatch*. (See Exhibit 2-1.)

Al fully expected his ad to work, but it did not. Al was the "operator standing by" mentioned in the ad. Thus, when he had received no calls at all by 4 p.m. on the day the ad was placed, he was sure his 800 phone number was not working. So, just to make sure, he had friends call him on it to test it. Unfortunately, it turned out that the number was working but the ad was not. In fact, the ultimate number of orders received was zero!

Al is now trying to figure out what happened and what, if anything, he should do next in his effort to sell vitamins by mail.

Questions

1. Analyze the ad shown in Exhibit 2-1 and the media in which it appeared for their consistency with good direct mail and direct marketing principles.

Materials in this case reprinted with permission of Kinser Pharmaceutical, Inc.

Exhibit 2-1 *Columbus Dispatch* Newspaper Advertisement

Introducing... **Bull Markets**

30 Day
Trial Offer

...an important **new** addition to your success.

Most executives and successful businessmen function at greater extremes than average people. The result is fatigue, your body weakening, etc...

Bull Markets is a powerful multivitamin/multimineral formula created to strengthen you, keep you ahead where you belong.

FDA aproved, the result of 30 years of vitamin experience, a combination of 25 essential vitamins and minerals with extra vitamins B¹, B², E, C, B₆, B₁₂, and iron, it's everything you need.

We'd like you to try a 30 day supply of Bull Markets. The cost is $5.00 plus $1.00 for shipping and, of course, a money back guarantee. A small price for your health

If you don't think you need Bull Markets to protect your health, to strengthen you, and to help you think clearer on long days... think again, and buy it before your competition does.

<u>Call Now!</u> Order Toll Free, Operator Standing By. 1-800-426-4010

MasterCard or Visa accepted. Please give your number to operator when calling.

or send coupon

One bottle at $5.00, plus $1.00 handing. Enclose check, money order, or MC No.
Two bottles (one for a friend) save $1.00. Total for two is $11.00

Name _____ MasterCard or Visa No

Address: _____ Zip Code

Send To: **Kinser Pharmaceutical Inc.**
P.O. Box 211, National Rd.
Englewood, Ohio 45325

•Limited while trial samples last.

2. Are vitamins a good direct-response channel product? Explain.
3. Discuss the positioning and offer used by Al Binkley.
4. Develop a total direct-response strategy for selling vitamins that you think will work.

Case 3

Select Communications, Inc. (SCI)

Introducing and Selling a New Service by Mail

Select Communications, Inc. (SCI) is a telecommunications consulting firm formed in December 1993 to obtain discounted long-distance telephone rates for small and medium-sized commercial end users.

In the 1980s, changes in Federal Communications Commission (FCC) tariffs provided for volume and contract pricing tariffs. Specialized application of these tariffs pertaining to long-distance carrier networks, such as AT&T, US Sprint, MCI Communications, Metro Media, and Wiltel, makes it possible for SCI to get clients long-distance rates comparable to those for the "Fortune 500." In effect, SCI clients pay the rates they would be paying if they were assessed long-distance telephone charges under long-distance carriers' volume rate structures.

SCI is paid on a commission basis. The amount of commission SCI receives depends on the volume of long-distance charges of a given company, and the type of service that is discounted. The different types of services that are discounted include 800 inbound, outbound, hospitality, and WATS line systems.

Initially, the company's income is limited to commissions based on total volume of business collected in each product category. As the company grows and gains experience, it plans to have a portion of its income derived from consulting fees for selective products and clients.

SCI's marketing approach uses a combination of direct mail and telemarketing. Prospective customers will be sent the following letter advising them of an opportunity to reduce their phone bill. It is hoped that the letter provides the encouragement needed for the customer to respond by returning the postcard. Upon receipt of the returned card, SCI plans to phone the customer's designated contact person to determine his or her billing and rates.

The letter shown in Exhibit 3-1 was the initial effort at creating a sell piece for the service. After discussing the concept and letter with a person with some direct response experience, the letter was revised as shown in Exhibit 3-2.

Exhibit 3-1   SCI's Initial Letter

Dear Prospect:

Your company may qualify for a 20 percent to 40 percent reduction in long-distance charges (depending on your telephone usage). Recent changes in Federal Communications Commission tariffs now make this possible while you continue to use your current carrier (AT&T, MCI, or Sprint).

SCI enables small and medium-sized companies to obtain lower long-distance rates formerly reserved for only the "Fortune 500" companies! By combining your long-distance usage with thousands of other cost-conscious firms, you achieve volume tariff savings that are otherwise impossible to receive on your own.

To learn how you can get an immediate reduction, complete and return the enclosed card today.

There are no additional costs or fees related to this service. Due to the high volume of requests received, your card will be processed on a first-come, first-served basis.

If you have any questions about this program, you may call (513) 233-9922.

Sincerely,

Denise M. Murlin
Telecommunications Consultant

Questions

1. Evaluate the overall strategy of SCI beginning with an evaluation of whether there is a need for the service.
2. Evaluate the structure (one-step direct mail) of the marketing strategy selected and the specifics of the letter that is being used. Will it work or not, and why? Make recommendations.

The authors wish to gratefully acknowledge contributing author Denise Murlin of Select Communications, Inc.

Exhibit 3-2   SCI's Revised Letter

Dear Prospect:

Your company may qualify for a 20 percent to 40 percent reduction in long distance charges (depending on your telephone usage). Recent changes in Federal Communications Commission tariffs now make this possible while you continue to use your current carrier (AT&T, MCI, or Sprint).

SCI helps customers with long-distance bills between $50 and $10,000 obtain significant savings while continuing to use the major long-distance networks. SCI is a telecommunications consulting firm designed to help small and medium-sized companies stop overpaying for long-distance phone service.

Here's how it works:

Small to medium-sized companies' long-distance usage is pooled to get volume discount rates. This gives them access to low rates formerly reserved for only the "Fortune 500" companies.

   Example of savings: 20 percent off of a $75 monthly average long-distance bill will give you a savings of $180 per year.

These extraordinary volume tariff savings are impossible for clients to get on their own—without the benefit of the group's volume. We provide this service without charging you a fee.

To learn how you can get an immediate reduction, complete and return the enclosed card today either by mail or FAX to (513) 233-8898.

If you have any questions about this program, you may call (513) 233-9922.

Sincerely,

Denise M. Murlin

Case 4

Dudes
Recruiting Dude Ranch Guests by Mail

Ernest and Julie Crandall made a mid-career move from Houston, Texas to the highlands of Colorado in 1978, where, together, they have operated a dude ranch—now known as Tomeche Hot Springs Ranch—for nearly fifteen years.

It had taken all their savings to buy what at the time was a run-down cattle ranch in the Colorado highlands, but it was everything they had ever hoped for. The ranch sat at the bottom of Tomeche Dome, an inactive volcano, whose geothermal action fed a variety of ground springs with a year-around, unlimited supply of 105-degree water. One of these springs was less than a hundred yards from the ranch house. The ranch was also near the Continental Divide, 45 minutes by van from scenic grandeur that rivaled that available any-where on the North American continent. It was also located near abandoned gold mines and historic, but no longer used, railway tun-nels through the Rocky Mountains. Furthermore, the ranch was near the back side of the "Vail" slope which offered, according to skiing afi-cionados, the best snow skiing in Colorado.

Ernest and Julie had not set out to become dude ranchers, but be-came involved in the business as a way to make ends meet early on in their adventure. The geographic setting of the ranch and the need for extra money combined to encourage Ernest and Julie to try the business in summer of 1980. They liked it immediately and found it relatively easy to manage, with Ernest handling the outdoor opera-tions and Julie handling the hotel, food-service, and marketing as-pects of the operation. Over the years, they prospered and built the business into one that produced a very good living for themselves and their three sons—all now young adults—who were ages 2, 3, and 5 when they came to the mountains.

All three boys, Rob, Les, and Ron, were now bright, outgoing young men, all of whom had gone off to college, but who, having grown up on the ranch and in the mountains—loving it all the while—wanted to make it their life's work. Rob, the oldest, and Les, the second son, were already married, and Ron and his fiance were planning their wedding. The wives were all very supportive of their husbands staying on the ranch and felt that they, too, could combine marriage and careers of their own by participating in the dude ranching business with their husbands. The only question was whether dude ranching could support them.

The ranch set-up could now accommodate 40 families of up to 6 people at a time—$550.00 per person being the average weekly rate. An average of 25 families visited the ranch each week during the summer season. Business for the horse-riding aspects of the ranch operation was very seasonal—limited largely to the summer months of June, July, and August. Hunting and skiing activities offered by the ranch were largely fall and winter activities.

Over the years repeat business and business from recommendations of satisfied customers were the primary basis of the business's growth. Essentially all the marketing Julie did was to send a very personal, homey letter and brochure to former visitors telling them of happenings on the ranch and inviting them back for another visit. She was also supplied with leads by the Colorado Department of Tourism when they got general inquiries about vacationing opportunities in Colorado. These were mailed a brochure—the same one that went to former customers—and a price list.

The happenings Julie talked about in her correspondence with former customers were largely personal items about individuals in the Crandall family, or if not that, about developments at the ranch, such as the completion of a new stable or the addition of a new attraction for their guests.

Every ranch visitor was made very welcome by the entire family. All of the ranch employees, including non-family members, acted less like employees of the ranch than they did friends and informal leaders to the ranch visitors/guests. In fact, the entire operation was conducted in a manner that left virtually all visitors with the feeling of having had a very entertaining, carefree visit with the Crandall family, rather than merely having spent a carefree week at a facility in the mountains.

The entire week (a week being the typical stay) was conducted as if one big family were together having a good time—on mountain-top horseback rides, van trips to mountain passes and abandoned gold mines, chuck-wagon breakfasts, riding the rapids of the Gunnison river on rafts, overnight campouts in mountain canyons, fishing trips to nearby trout streams, or just lounging around the ranch's geothermally heated, 105-degree pool and waiting for the next all-you-can-eat meal cooked under the supervision of a lady who earned her reputation cooking for hardy Colorado goldminers.

But now things were changing. More people were getting into the dude ranch business—and doing a better job at it. Furthermore, if all of the Crandall sons and their families were to earn their living on the ranch, business would have to be sought much more vigorously.

Questions

1. What is the major problem in this case?
2. Would the Crandalls benefit from understanding database marketing?
3. Is the structure of the program needed by the Crandalls materially different than that needed by any direct marketer?
4. Develop a direct-response strategy for the Crandall family that will increase the operation's business—first to present capacity, then to whatever capacity you feel is merited in this particular situation.

Case 5

Letters

Putting Some Direct-Response Sizzle into Letters

With one exception, the letters displayed in Exhibits 5-1, 5-2, 5-3, and 5-4 do not take a direct marketing posture as they deliver their messages. Rewrite each letter that does not reflect direct marketing principles, putting as much direct-response technology into them as you feel is appropriate. Evaluate the probable effectiveness of the letter with the greatest direct marketing flavor.

Exhibit 5-1   Outerbelt Center Letter

To: Merchants
Re: Outerbelt Center Downgrading

Time and time again I have written the merchants about downgrading the shopping center, criticizing the landlord, and in other ways undercutting your own livelihood here.

Every time a prospective tenant walks around the Mall and talks to the merchants, all he ever gets is criticism. Don't you realize the criticism is hurting you? I realize that there are many of you who are not doing well and who would rather blame me for your own inadequacies than your own inability to operate a business properly. If you want to do that, there is nothing that says you can't write me about it or even tell me about it personally. But why would you run down even your own place of business? Although an obvious effort to get at me, this only results in your cutting off your nose to spite your face.

Prospective tenants come and tell me they have talked to the merchants and from what they hear from the merchants, they do not feel they want to come into the shopping center. If that is what you want, I can assure you that it will happen. They will not come into the shopping center, stores will be vacant, and I will not get any additional rent, but remember, you will lose sales because vacancies are not a compliment to a shopping center.

And another thing. I do not ever want to hear any merchant ask me, "Why don't you rent vacant stores?" You know why, so do not ask me. I do not want to hear about it.

Yours very truly,

Sidney J. Bromley

SJB:mv
CC: Main office

Exhibit 5-2   New Products Incorporated Letter

New Products Incorporated
Box 256
Iowa City, Indiana 54680

Dear President:

The Tat'l Tail safety flag which is described on the attached brochure is an excellent premium item. Many Savings & Loans are using it to promote bicycle safety and at the same time promote thrift among their people. They work with local police departments and fraternal organizations to provide public safety campaigns. Many times these are done through the school system, and the group will present a safety program and follow it up with an offer allowing each of the students to come into their Savings & Loan and pick up a Tat'l Tail safety flag as either a gift or a premium for saving.

We've designed the Tat'l Tail to be a high-quality item. The pennant (sample enclosed) is made of vinyl impregnated nylon, resistant to weathering, tattering, tearing, fading, and stretching, and is permanently attached to the fiberglass whiprod. A unique attachment holds the rod securely to prevent theft and can be attached to almost any vehicle such as bicycles, snowmobiles, motorcycles, and agricultural equipment. If you compare the Tat'l Tail with other similar products, you will find it to be the best.

Our normal terms of sale call for full payment within 30 days of shipping. We will ship by the most convenient method and will add freight to the purchase price or bill it collect. To place your order, just fill out the attached order blank and send it to the address listed below. We will be looking forward to your order, and we wish you the best with the Tat'l Tail safety flag.

New Products Incorporated
Box 256
Iowa City, Indiana 54680

Exhibit 5-3   Heating and Air Conditioning Inc.

Haircor Heating Co.
1251 Weton Center
Palantine, Nebraska

Gentlemen:

Enclosed is our latest illustrated and descriptive catalog sheet of items we manufacture.

Haircor products have been successfully manufactured and installed for over 25 years.

The Haircor Silencers are manufactured in various sizes. They eliminate the problem of hammering in water lines.

In keeping with the present fuel oil shortages, it is to the advantage of the consumer to have installed Haircor motorized zone controlled gate valves, which help keep fuel consumption down. Specific zoning sections in residential or commercial buildings can be heated when necessary. This too is a savings in fuel costs.

The Haircor fuel oil tank gauge will show at a glance the amount of fuel oil in the tank regardless of its location. This gauge should be installed at the same time of the tank installation.

For satisfaction and excellence in performance, specify Haircor Products.

Kindly contact your wholesale distributor for further information.

Sincerely yours,

                                                            Haircor Heating Co.
                                                            1251 Weton Center
                                                            Palantine, Nebraska

Exhibit 5-4   Frank Helbig's Job Hunt

800 South Wacker, Apt. 710
Chicago, Illinois 60607

Are you looking for a
Senior Direct Marketing
Manager? Like one that
took a start-up situation
to $60 million in sales in
nine years!

...If you are, I think you'll want to use the enclosed postage-paid reply card
to learn more about a seasoned pro who could be <u>very valuable</u> to your company.

This person developed and implemented direct marketing programs for
a manufacturer of big-ticket consumer power tools when distribution
through a dealer network became unprofitable. The results...<u>sales grew
from $3 million dollars to $60 million in 9 years</u>. He managed a sales and
marketing staff that went from 3 to 285. He's a hands-on manager who's
experienced with lists, space, creative, direct mail, telemarketing, television,
catalogs. He's even developed and integrated a retail network into the
direct marketing sales channels.

In short, this guy <u>knows direct marketing from A to Zip</u>! As you
may have guessed, the person I'm describing is myself. If you
are looking for a talented senior direct marketing manager, I
feel I have a lot to offer. What's more, I'm prepared to prove it
with a <u>SPECIAL FREE OFFER</u>.

I don't expect you to thoroughly evaluate my talents by the few paragraphs
above, but I'll be happy to send you an <u>interesting, detailed resume</u>. Look it
over and see if there isn't a place for my talents in your company...or with
someone you know.

To get the resume, just complete and return the postage-paid reply card
enclosed. Or, for even faster action, you can phone me at 312-431-3384.

Sincerely yours,

Frank Helbig

P.S.   Since I'm presently employed I've used a pseudonym for
        confidentiality.

Case 6

Magna Deca
Test Marketing a Consumer Durable

The home fitness equipment market was continuing to grow, and the success in particular, of direct marketers in the field attracted the attention of Jim Sherwood, the marketing manager of Magna Deca, a larger consumer goods company. Jim's company marketed largely through traditional channels, but wanted to get into direct response and felt it had found an appropriate product.

The product was an at-home physical fitness product selling for less than $500. Magna Deca had acquired the product and was prepared to give it the necessary marketing push if the market appeared to be there, but only if it was "there" in the direct-response channel. To find out, Jim Sherwood commissioned a local direct-response advertising firm to come up with a test direct marketing plan. The plan that the company suggested involved simultaneous testing of four positioning concepts and five magazines from five different media groupings—all at the same time. The names of 20,000 subscribers of five different magazines were to be rented and one quarter of each of these 20,000-subscriber sets were to be exposed to one of four positioning concepts. (See Table 6-1.)

It was decided that 5,000 subscribers from each test magazine would be mailed a lead-generating piece built around each of four positioning themes. In this way it was felt that both the media and the message could be tested at once. The test program was to be run under the name Personal Fitness Systems (PFS), rather than the Magna Deca name.

These four positioning themes are contained in the following headlines for four different self-mailers:

1. $500 won't pay for much medical care, but it could buy a lifetime of better health.
2. You don't have to spend hours jogging to get the exercise you really need.
3. Give your family the benefits of a complete $40,000 gym...for less than $500!
4. The Million Dollar Body...for less than $500!

Table 6-1   Simultaneous Concept and Magazine Test

		Positioning Concepts			
Publication Category	Test Magazine	Body Building	Health Improvement	Alternative to Jogging	Family Gym
Business and Travel	*Businessweek*	5000	5000	5000	5000
Men's Publications	*Playboy*	5000	5000	5000	5000
Sports Publications	*Sports Illustrated*	5000 .	5000	5000	5000
Science and Electronics	*Mechanics Illustrated*	5000	5000	5000	5000
News Weeklies	*Time*	5000	5000	5000	5000

Questions

1. Is the family gym a viable direct-response product?
2. What are some of the possible motivations for buying the family gym, and how do these relate to positioning?
3. What lists or media appear to be appropriate?
4. Evaluate this testing program and suggest other approaches that might have been more appropriate and/or more effective in this situation.

Materials in this case used by permission of SEI.

Case 7

Workmate, Inc.
Solving Intra-channel Pricing Conflicts

Workmate, Inc. sells a multipurpose woodworking tool. Initially, this product was sold in shopping malls using on-site demonstrations by factory sales personnel. This very successful strategy was then complemented with a direct mail program designed to sell people who expressed interest at the malls but did not buy there, and to sell people who inquired as a result of magazine and other types of advertising. Still later, a telephone marketing program was added to the program structure.

All of Workmate's marketing effort melded together quite well with the exception of its price quotation program.

Mall sales teams sold the product for $1,195 and induced buyers to "buy now" with a $100 discount if the buyer purchased during the demonstration period (teams usually spent one week in each mall, then moved on).

The direct mail group found the "$100 off for a limited time only" strategy effective and ran such programs periodically. The direct mail inquiree was sent a package of promotional materials among which was a $100 coupon good for 60 days.

Approximately 14 days before the coupon discount period ended (coupons were stamped), the telemarketing group took over and attempted to sell the prospect on placing an order before the 60 days were up. This program was only marginally effective, so the telemarketing group was permitted to offer an additional $50 inducement to buy now. This worked well.

The problem was that inquirers frequently turned up at malls holding a $100 discount coupon and, also, were frequently aware of an additional $50 discount if they ordered via the telephone, making it difficult for mall teams to make their $100 inducement to "buy now" effective.

This problem got a lot of study, and one conclusion was that the mall teams must always have the lowest and best offer—that is, the lowest price of the three channels. The problem was how to accomplish this.

Questions

1. Why do buyers buy through different channels?

2. Why does intra-channel conflict occur?
3. What are the requirements for effective price discrimination?
4. What do you think can be done to solve this channel conflict?

Case 8   Complete Petmart
Battling the Pet Supply Superstore Invasion with Direct Marketing

The battle for market share among large pet supply chains is creating competitive turbulence in the entire pet supply channel. Independent "mom and pop" retailers are being replaced by larger and more sophisticated chain operators. Some of these chains have grown into regional players with up to 25 locations and a presence in 3 and 4 contiguous states, and a few have grown in scope and size to include up to 150 operations in 20 or more states. All of these large chains operate superstore formats in sizes ranging from 6,000 to 25,000 square feet. They sell cat, dog, and other pet food as well as almost every toy, treat, shampoo, leash, cage, or novelty a pet owner could want.

A current head-to-head battle for market share among these large pet supply superstore chains is rapidly increasing the level of competitive tension, not only among the superstores themselves but also between the superstores and the remaining "mom and pops" and smaller regional pet supply chains. According to some observers, the superstore competition is entering the "terror" stage: that is, "you tear at my profits and I'll tear at yours until we both experience sheer agony." The current focus of this competitive struggle is on selected premium pet food items or "SKUs" (stock-keeping units).

Some superstore chains have decided that premium pet food will be the weapon of choice in their battle for market share. Premium pet food is the product line that allowed pet supply retailers of all types to succeed in the pet supply business and differentiate themselves from grocery stores. Premium pet foods have permitted pet supply retailers to realize profit margins of approximately 25 percent and often contributed over 30 percent of the total gross profit earned by pet supply stores. Without the profit afforded by these products, the large superstores, and everyone else in the pet supply industry, will have a difficult time operating in the black.

Complete Petmart, a successful and still-growing 10-store regional pet supply chain in Ohio, is one of a number of small chains across the country that is bracing for the entrance of a national superstore chain, PetsMart, into its market. Complete Petmart operates in three Ohio markets—Cincinnati, Columbus, and Dayton; its stores are in the lower superstore range, averaging about 7,000 square feet. PetsMart's entry into all three of Complete Petmart's markets will take place when it completes its acquisition of Petzazz, a 30-store chain that currently competes in all of Complete Petmart's markets. Petzazz stores will be renamed and become PetsMart stores.

Complete Petmart and PetsMart differ more in the number of shelf facings (different sizes, brands, etc.) than in the total number of items (kinds of products) carried—PetsMart superstores have about 7,000 SKUs compared with Complete Petmart's 4,000. With their much greater number of facings, PetsMart stores look big and "bargainy." Neither Complete Petmart nor PetsMart sells live "companion animal" pets. Both sell fish and related paraphernalia and both feature premium companion-animal foods produced by such well-known firms as Iams, Nutro, and Hill—companies that built the premium pet food market from scratch in the late 1970s and 1980s. Neither company sells "grocery-store" pet food brands such as Friskies, Purina Chow, Alpo, Tender Vittles, Ken-L Ration, or Mighty Dog. Grocery stores, once the dominant outlet for pet food, now sell less than two-thirds of the industry's total $8.4 billion in sales.[4] The premium brands now account for 22 percent of total pet food sales.[5] The average lifetime upkeep for a pet can be in the $10,000 range over the life of a typical pet. (See Exhibit 8-1.)

Complete Petmart's merchandising strategy includes a 6½ inventory turns per year target compared with 2½ turns for the giant PetsMart superstores. Complete Petmart has a policy of 100 percent in-stock on 85 popular pet supply items. The company has a heavy service strategy with the bulk of its service being provided by employees 16 to 21 years of age who are earning "car money" for the most part. Employee turnover is high; thus, training is continuous and expensive.

Complete Petmart attempts to develop a relationship with pet owners through such activities as taking and posting pictures of owners and pets, sending birthday cards to pets, and offering significant discounts to specific pets on their birthdays. PetsMart does these things too, but much less elaborately and for strategically different seasons. PetsMart offers an adoption program for pets. Also, like Complete Petmart, PetsMart's customers can bring in their pets for photos with Santa and for Easter egg hunts (with smelly treats helping the dogs track down the plastic eggs). This program gives PetsMart the appearance of offering elaborate relationship-building and consumer services, but the actuality is much less than the appearance.

---

[4]*Advertising Age*, April 25, 1994, p. 42.
[5]*Ibid.*

Exhibit 8-1   How Much Is That Doggie in the Window? Try $11,580

Adopting a pet may seem like a modest investment. In fact, the financial
commitment is quite steep. And that doesn't include all the little extras…

	Cat	Dog
The Down Payment		
Adopting a pet	$25	$55
Having it "fixed"	50	70
First year vaccination	200	200
License	5	10
Training	—	75
Total one-time costs	$280	$410
Annual Upkeep		
Vaccinations	$35	$65
Toys and grooming	75	210
Boarding—2 weeks	140	300
Food	152	257
Kitty litter	77	—
Veterinary care	80	135
Professional haircuts	—	150
Total annual costs	$559	$1,117
Assumes average life span	15 years	10 years
Total Bare-bones lifetime costs	$8,665	$11,580

Source: Humane Society of the United States. *The New York Times*, Sept. 11, 1994 (Section 3).

PetsMart clearly wants to have the lowest price all the time, but it
wants to portray itself as the neighborhood pet store as well. Pets-
Mart operates in an overall manner designed to maximize distribution efficiency and, therefore, operate at minimum costs.

Before the mid-1970s, pet food was a by-product of consumer cereal manufacturing, made from cereal that did not get processed sep-
arately. Thus, pet food was relatively cheap compared to modern
premium pet food, which is designed for pets and which offers a variety of attractive benefits to pets and pet owners in exchange for a
premium price. Traditionally, pet food was sold in a grocery store.
Modern premium pet food distribution is largely limited to pet supply stores, veterinarians, and the like, where the price premium the
food commands can be explained.

Distributors are major players in the premium pet food industry.
They became prominent in the early stages of market development,
initially serving the "pet lover" turned merchant, and evolved to
served more sophisticated retail operations. To date, the major premium pet food suppliers have refused to sell direct to anyone but

the overwhelmingly large superstores; thus, Complete Petmart still buys Iams, Hill, and Nutro products from distributors, while Pets-Mart bypasses distributors and buys direct.

As in most industries, pet food wholesale prices are quoted as discounts from suggested retail, with distributors' margins at 9 percent. PetsMart buys direct and gets a 5 percent discount. Iams will not cut its price to small buyers but does offer a theoretically matching 4 percent cooperative advertising discount as long as the money is used to advertise products priced above specified minimum levels.

Complete Petmart stores tend to be located adjacent to affluent neighborhoods, and therefore offer convenience, while PetsMart stores tend to locate in high-traffic "power centers" where so-called "category killers" such as Wickes, Toys 'R Us, and so on locate.

In other markets it has entered, PetsMart's strategy has been to establish itself as a price leader. For example, it has been known to put a 40-pound bag of Hill's Science Diet Maintenance dog food, which costs the company approximately $22.00, on sale for $18.99. Complete Petmart's everyday retail price for this item is $29.95, and its cost is approximately $23.50.

Don Laden, President of Complete Petmart, is preparing his organization for the new competitive environment. He has already decided that competing head-to-head with PetsMart on price will not be successful. Furthermore, he does not believe that matching Pets-Mart's pricing is necessary because there is, he believes, a commercially large price-insensitive market that seeks and will pay for truly outstanding pet supply-related services if they are the right services and if they are promoted correctly. Mr. Laden believes that he must involve his company in modern one-on-one marketing, database marketing, and other service-quality–related marketing approaches to whatever degree is necessary to minimize cost objections while maximizing pet owner–firm partnering.

Questions

1. What overall promotion strategy should be undertaken to support a premium product and price policy for Complete Petmart?
2. Identify some of the specifics of a one-on-one and database-driven promotion program that will be needed to support a premium product and price policy for Complete Petmart.
3. Rank order in terms of importance and explain the role of 10 price sensitivity factors as these are used by buyers of pet food, and by Complete Petmart's buyers in particular.

4. What type of pricing behavior does it appear that PetsMart will engage in when it enters Complete Petmart's market? Give a brief but clear reason for your choice.

5. If Complete Petmart is forced to lower its overall price level by 25 percent in order to compete with PetsMart, how much will its volume have to increase for Complete Petmart to be as profitable as it is at present—assuming that Complete Petmart's costs are typically 60 percent of price?

6. If Complete Petmart has research information showing that about half of its customer base is significantly price insensitive, exactly what has the research revealed? Be precise in your answer.

7. If Complete Petmart responds to the apparent competitive threat posed by PetsMart appropriately, what is the first thing that the company will do?

8. What are the relative roles of value, competition, and costs in the pricing of pet food and pet supply market products?

9. What, apparently, is the basic pricing strategy that Complete Petmart is currently using?

10. Outline a marketing and pricing strategy for Complete Petmart as it readies itself for the competitive onslaught that appears to be headed its way.

11. What are the financial implications of Complete Petmart's 6½ stock turns versus 2½ stock turns by PetsMart.

12. Your task is to outline a one-on-one, database, quality management program designed to accomplish Mr. Laden's goals.

The authors wish to gratefully acknowledge Complete Petmart President Don Laden for his cooperation and assistance in the development of this case.

Case 9

Helzberg Diamonds Shops, Inc.

Building a Retail Customer Base

Early History

Morris Helzberg opened the first Helzberg jewelry store, a 12-foot store front in Kansas City, Kansas, in 1915. The Helzberg Diamonds shop may have been a small force of the day, but it was established with high principles that would predicate phenomenal growth.

Morris's young son, B.C., enjoyed spending Saturdays in his father's tiny store. But when Morris suffered a stroke just a few years later, B.C. found himself responsible for the entire operation. As was the practice in those days, Helzberg Diamonds carried silverware, eyeglasses, china, crystal, and small appliances in addition to jewelry.

Young B.C. loved the store. He often dreamed of selling diamonds and jewelry in stores across the Midwest. And it wasn't long before his dreams began to come true. By 1929, B.C. had expanded to four locations, adding stores in Kansas City, Missouri and in Wichita and Topeka, Kansas.

The Helzberg Diamonds shops were highly respected businesses that gave time and money back to their communities. As an entrepreneur B.C. was so confident that he went beyond defying the miserable economy of the Great Depression. He doubled the size of his Kansas City, Missouri store in 1932. The Helzberg "Sweetheart Hour" on WDAF radio was welcome, uplifting entertainment and relief to the Kansas City community in the 1930s.

B.C. Helzberg was well on his way to success when World War II rocked the country and the world. As the war came to a close, B.C. added two more stores so he could employ returning servicemen. By 1947, Helzberg Diamonds consisted of eight stores in three states: Missouri, Kansas, and Iowa. Living always on the leading edge, Helzberg Diamonds was one of the first to offer customers the luxury of air conditioning.

In 1950, Helzberg Diamonds showcased the legendary Hope Diamond and donated all proceeds to the campaign to fight polio. The early fifties saw further expansions of the Helzberg organization as the seventh store opened in the Greater Kansas City area, bringing the company total to twelve. Helzberg Diamonds was indeed well on its way to becoming the Middle West's largest jeweler. In 1956, Barnett

C. Helzberg, Jr. joined Helzberg Diamonds as the third generation in the family firm.

Barnett began the mail-order sales of Helzberg Diamonds' non-jewelry product lines. In 1963, Barnett was given the responsibility of leading the company and making his own impression on the industry and the community, following in the footsteps of his father and grandfather. When Barnett took the helm, Helzberg Diamonds operated 39 stores.

His first major order of business was the repositioning of Helzberg Diamonds stores, phasing out of downtown areas and expanding into major shopping malls. In 1967, Helzberg Diamonds opened its first corner store in a shopping mall, a move that characterizes the company today. Its success was immediate, and Helzberg Diamonds has added mall stores every year since. 1967 was also the year that Barnett Helzberg, Jr. created the *I am loved* slogan. The public adored the message, and Helzberg Diamonds became nationally recognized for the campaign. Buttons with the *I am loved* slogan have been given to educational programs to build the self-esteem of their students. Since its beginning, the company has distributed more than 25 million *I am loved* buttons, printed in six different languages, throughout the world. In the late 1970s, Helzberg Diamonds began focusing on its most important products—diamonds, fine gems, and karat gold jewelry—which was quite a refinement from its early days, which also included silverware, eyeglasses, china, crystal, and small appliances.

Recent Marketing Strategy

Helzberg Diamonds, as has always been the case, is customer oriented: it has well-trained, knowledgeable, polite, and well-treated employees who understand the importance of its customers. Its customer service has always been unmatched. Its current product lines are deeper than those of its most direct competitors.

Another strength is its quality control program, which carefully and affectionately inspects each and every piece of jewelry at six different stages before it finds its way into a Helzberg Diamonds showcase. The exceptional quality of not only its products but also its overall operation has led to "The Helzberg Guarantee" shown in Exhibit 9-1.

Helzberg Diamonds' target market is the middle- and upper-middle-income jewelry customer. Through experience it has found that its target market is reached most efficiently through strategic site locations in dominant retail centers, primarily center court, corner locations in major shopping center malls. Helzberg Diamonds successfully integrates inviting storefronts and innovative store dis-

Exhibit 9-1   The Helzberg Guarantee

YOU ARE GUARANTEED
the right to a full refund within 90 days.

YOU ARE GUARANTEED
to receive a Lifetime Diamond Guarantee
with every diamond and precious
gemstone purchase.

YOU ARE GUARANTEED
the right to polite service.

YOU ARE GUARANTEED
Helzberg personnel will be knowledgeable
about their merchandise.

YOU ARE GUARANTEED
Helzberg will always stand behind
its merchandise.

YOU ARE GUARANTEED
the right to object to
unsatisfactory merchandise.

YOU ARE GUARANTEED
the right to exceptional value and service
at all times.

plays to develop appealing atmospheres for gift shopping. Combined with an open environment of warm colors, the stores' ambiance invites casual browsing and encourages thoughtful buying. Rich cherry wood accents, jewelry cases, and art deco and handsome marble columns and floors clearly create an environment of service and quality.

Helzberg Diamonds has successfully diversified into a leading gift-giving retailer. Its advertising and promotional programs have always reflected an aggressive yet fun approach to reaching its target audience while communicating the joy of gift-giving. Helzberg Diamonds, for years, has effectively utilized a combination of broadcast, newspaper, and point-of-sale sign advertising to differentiate itself from the competition and to attract customers and build store traffic throughout the year. Its successful promotional programs are designed to draw customers into the store, while its unrivaled selection and affordable pricing motivate customers to purchase, and most importantly, return for future purchases for all occasions. Its 1994 Valentine's Day customer catalog, for example, advertised products that ranged in price from $19 (a 7" freshwater pearl and 14 karat gold bead bracelet) to $1,399 (a multi-diamond 14 karat gold band ring). The 107 products in that catalog had an average selling price of $251.30.

The Industry

With two exceptions, the above description could have described Helzberg Diamonds' marketing strategy in 1980 or in 1994 with equal accuracy. The first exception is a change in the scope of its operation. In the last 15 years, Helzberg Diamonds has quadrupled its number of stores from 34 to 133, and has increased its market presence to 23 states. Amazingly, during the hard economic times of the early 1990s, it increased the number of its retail outlets from 99 in 1990 to 133 in 1993.

This increase in the scope of the operations of Helzberg Diamonds may seem surprising during a time of worldwide economic recession, increasing competition, and the impact of political strategies on the industry. Worldwide retail diamond jewelry sales are estimated to be $39 billion, of which 29 percent (or $11.3 billion) are in the United States. Precious metal jewelry unit sales are expected to grow 4 percent annually through 1997.

Although economic downturns tend to shift lower-income jewelry buyers toward lower-price items, the number of purchases does not decrease. However, those downturns do not seem to affect the purchases of jewelry by higher-income buyers. Also, declines in economic activity and consumer confidence have their biggest effects on big-ticket items such as homes and automobiles, on discretionary items such as furniture, and on items bought on credit, but they have very little effect on small purchases such as appliances, food eaten at home, or personal care items. A limited insulation, relative to other retail industries, from huge business-cycle–induced sales fluctuations is also true for products such as perfume, chocolates, and flowers, all of which have also been traditionally associated with romance. Self-indulgence, fantasy, and leisure are at the heart of the romantic sell. The working woman's fantasy is to "have it all" without being completely consumed by work. To be effective, advertisements portraying successful women have been changing to reflect women's changing impressions of themselves. And Helzberg Diamonds' ads have continually changed with the times.

Even the since-rescinded 1990 Revenue Reconciliation Act luxury tax levied on automobiles over $30,000, boats over $100,000, aircraft over $250,000, and jewelry and furs over $10,000 failed to break the jewelry industry's partial insulation from the business cycle, primarily because of the act's short life, but also, for Helzberg Diamonds, because of its high dollar threshold.

But, as is true of any industry, the fortunes of an industry are not equally divided among its participants. Tiffany's, a name regarded by most to be synonymous with excellence in the industry, fell on hard times during the 1980s. Avon, which acquired Tiffany's in 1979, lengthened Tiffany's product lines to include more lower-priced items. In 1984, Tiffany's suffered a $5 million loss. Avon's strategy nearly destroyed Tiffany's name and reputation, leading to a leveraged buyout by its management. With a change back to its previous product mix strategy and an aggressive print-media advertising campaign, the new owners increased its sales from $230 million in 1988 to $502 million in 1992. But its largest international market, Japan, experienced a 35 percent sales decrease in that same year, causing Tiffany's earnings to drop 42 percent.

Several major retail jewelry companies encountered major financial difficulties in 1992. Zale Corporation, United States' largest jewelry retailer, and Barry's Jewelers Inc., the United States' third largest, both filed for Chapter 11 bankruptcy protection. Some other smaller retailers that encountered sales decreases closed some of their marginal stores and/or reduced inventories in stores that remained open. Although Helzberg Diamonds survived and thrived during the 1980s and the recession of the early 1990s, examples such as these indicate that it must continue to increase the effectiveness of its marketing efforts to avoid such problems itself.

Database Marketing

The other change in Helzberg Diamonds' marketing strategy over the last 15 years has been its movement into database marketing. With the switch of its product mix in the late 1970s to specialize in diamonds, fine gems, and karat gold jewelry, the other nonjewelry products sold by mail-order through its catalog were eliminated—and thus its mail-order catalog was also eliminated. But direct marketing was not eliminated.

In the late 1970s, Helzberg Diamonds had a hard-copy list of 20,000 to 30,000 customers. Although in great disarray, that original customer list formed the basis for Helzberg Diamonds move into the era of sophisticated, computerized database marketing.

Although the development of its new direct marketing effort relies on many of the same principles that its original nonjewelry catalog did, its objectives differ. The objectives of its new catalog are to generate measurable store traffic, while at the same time capturing vital information about each consumer's buyer behavior and geodemography. This information includes recency, frequency, monetary (RFM), product SKU number, list, name and address, purchase occasion, credit card, and geodemographic enhancement data.

Daily, all Helzberg Diamonds stores submit the above information (except enhancement data) to Helzberg Diamonds' single master database. The capturing of the list data has grown the database to nearly 2 million customers in just 15 years. Address corrections are made periodically through National Change of Address (NCOA) matchings. Customers who move from one Helzberg Diamonds market area to another continue to received store catalogs on the basis of their RFMs and are given the address of the store nearest to their new residence.

Some other uses of the database include the following:

1. Profiling customers or certain types of customers to develop potential prospect profiles
2. Selecting a subsample of buyers who have certain attributes (first-time buyers, big spenders, holiday purchasers, etc.) to receive targeted catalogs
3. Determining markets that require additional promotional support
4. Determining markets that could support an additional Helzberg Diamonds store
5. Analyzing product sales by SKU, by catalog, by market, and/or by store

Helzberg Diamonds wishes to continue to increase the effective use of its database in making tactical marketing decisions. The company is considering using its database to promote birthday gift sales. In the United States, the biggest gift-giving holidays in the jewelry business are Christmas, Mother's Day, and Valentine's Day, in that order. But the next leading occasion for buying jewelry is birthdays, second only to Christmas.

Assume that Helzberg Diamonds has not yet set up or used its database for the purpose of promoting birthday gift sales. Also, for the purposes of this case, assume that Helzberg Diamonds considers customers to be active if they have purchased within the last 36 months.

Questions

1. What data would Helzberg Diamonds need to add to its database to adopt a database-driven birthday gift marketing strategy to generate in-store sales? (Note: disregard birthday presents purchased by the customer for himself or herself.)

2. How, and at what cost, would you obtain the data suggested in Question 1?
3. Develop an operational promotional campaign strategy for Helzberg Diamonds, using its database as modified under Questions 1 and 2, to better penetrate the jewelry industry's large birthday-gift–buying market.

This case was prepared by Richard A. Hamilton, Associate Professor of Direct Marketing, University of Missouri– Kansas City.

Case 10

PreFone Integrated Products, Inc.
Telemarketing a "Junk Phone Call" Screener

Dr. Robert Buchan, both a retired general practitioner and a trained engineer, has formed a company, PreFone Integrated Products, Inc. (PIP), to introduce and sell his first and future products. His current invention is a telephone device known as the PreFone Filter™ which protects consumers from unwanted telephone calls, specifically unsolicited telemarketing.

Dr. Buchan's invention is in response to his own discontent and anger with "junk" calls and his observance of the growing discontent of the public with this interruption of personal privacy. The increasing media attention to this problem as well as government concern in the form of proposed regulations stimulated his technological interests, and the result is a product that will stop the problem at the consumer's point of reception. The strength of his invention is the almost complete elimination of harassment to the consumer.

Dr. Buchan initiated development of his product by doing research into the rapidly growing telemarketing industry, the attitudes of consumers in reaction to the increase in junk calls, and the reaction of the government to concerns of the consumers.

Telemarketing Industry Facts

The telemarketing industry

- Includes an estimated 300,000 commercial sales solicitors making in excess of 18 million telemarketing telephone calls daily (Contact the Congressional Research Service Bureau for more information.)
- Is experiencing a 35 percent annual growth rate in the number of telemarketing calls
- Does better and does more calling in a sluggish or recessionary economy
- Does not want to call and talk to people who do not want to receive these calls (Long-distance line charges are based on 6-second blocks and conversation with angry, negative respondents is costly.)
- Often experiences 50 percent angry disconnects on successful contacts (Telephone sales representatives, or TSRs, are instructed to try to disconnect the line within the first 6 seconds on these calls.)
- Generally instructs its telephone sales representatives to disconnect immediately upon hearing a recorded voice (local telemar-

keters, charities, and other contribution seekers generally do the same).

The Consumer Market and Competition for the PreFone Filter™

Consumer attitudes have not been thoroughly studied by independent researchers; however, some of the studies that have been done are revealing. For example, in a major telephone company study of customer-reported "problem" calls over a 12-month period, 90 percent cent of the customers complained of too frequent sales and telemarketing calls. Ninety-three percent of customers reported dissatisfaction and irritation with misdial and hang-up calls. (Hang-up calls sometimes occur when telephone list purveyors are developing "at home" profiles of prospects). Twenty-nine percent reported one or more obscene calls. There was no difference in "problem" call percentages between listed and unlisted telephone subscribers.

"Caller I.D." (CID) and "Block the Blocker" are two services of the regional telephone companies (the "Baby Bells" plus GTE) in those states where they are authorized. These services are strictly targeted to limit unwanted "problem" calls and to reduce the frequency of obscene calls. More than 10,000 subscribers signed up for Caller I.D. service in New Jersey in the first year of operation. A subscriber to Caller I.D. purchases a "black box" for a fee and pays a monthly service charge. When the phone rings, a user goes to the telephone and observes the number displayed on the unit's LCD screen. If the number or area code is not recognized, the user may choose not to answer. For a monthly fee people are purchasing a service that requires them to go to the telephone when it rings and make a memory-based judgment that could result in unintended but serious consequences.

The service of per-call blocking is also available. In those states presently offering this service, an additional digit is added to the called number and this prevents the Caller I.D. "black box" from displaying the calling number on its screen, protecting the "privacy rights" of the caller! Unfortunately, this technology blocks all calls, not merely those that are unwanted. This means that emergency calls from pay phones, operator-assisted calls, credit card calls, and calls from agencies such as police departments, medical offices, etc., will also be blocked. It is also possible for a subscriber to purchase a Block the Blocker service which will present a recorded message to the call blocker indicating why the subscribers have not answered.

The "Baby Bells," GTE, and AT&T are all actively marketing these services. These firms may also be working on products directly competitive with PreFone Filter; however, none are known at this point by Dr. Buchan. Furthermore, he feels that his patent will protect him from any closely related device.

Telemarketing Legislation

About two-thirds of the 50 states have antitelemarketing legislation pending in one form or another. Because these are intrastate restrictions, they do not significantly affect the majority of telemarketing sources, which are large multistate, multinational corporations.

The Telephone Consumer Protection Act, TCPA, (Public Law 102–243), which went into effect on December 20, 1992, placed several restrictions on calls made to residences for the purpose of solicitation. Specifically, it requires callers to put a callee's name on a "do not call" list for 5 years when so instructed by the callee. Violators can be made to pay the callee from $500 to $1500. FCC regulations now stipulate telephone harassment as a civil penalty offense. Someone who calls, after having been specifically instructed not to do so, has violated an individual's civil right to privacy and is guilty of harassment. Another important restriction limits the time permitted for calls from 8:00 a.m. to 9:00 p.m. It should be noted, however, that among others exempt from the law are nonprofit organizations, charities, politicians, and pollsters.

The law also applies to the use of autodialers or prerecorded voice messages. Its intent is to allow such calls only in emergency situations or with prior consent of the resident. It prohibits calls to certain parties, such as emergency telephone lines and hospital patient rooms, and it prohibits any service in which the called party is charged for the call. It also requires identification of the caller at the beginning of the message, including address and telephone number. In May of 1993, however, a federal judge declared the regulations governing the use of autodialed recorded message players as outlined in the TCPA to be unconstitutional, essentially on the grounds that the regulations hinder commercial free speech.[6]

Included in the TCPA are regulations regarding proper facsimile usage. Essentially, the law does not allow anyone to transmit a solicitation without the prior consent of the receiving party. To enforce this, it requires facsimile machines manufactured after December 20, 1992 to have the capacity to mark identifying information on the transmission.

The telephone utility and long-line sellers' lobby is one of the most powerful and well-funded on Capitol Hill; thus, legislation that

---

[6]Kerr, Angela, "Legislative Update," *Teleprofessional,* July/August 1993, p. 6.

stops telemarketers from making calls to individual homes is not expected to succeed in Congress in the foreseeable future. (The reader should note that major new federal and state legislation in process at the time of this writing may enhance or reduce the viability of strategic alternatives in this case.) In view of this political situation, the only realistic way of stopping commercial calls is to stop them at individual telephones of consumers. Enter PreFone Filter™.

The PreFone Filter™

The PreFone Filter™ fits between the user's answering machine (if one exists) or the phone and the incoming line. (The production model of the product is 6 inches long, 4 inches wide, and 1.5 inches thick.) Electronically, the design represents leading-edge 100 percent solid state technology. All components are manufactured by American companies.

The design specifications and performance criteria are the result of sustained research by Dr. Buchan into three areas:

1. The present state of telephone signal technology
2. The factors that sponsors of unsolicited telemarketing calls do not want to encounter during a telemarketing call
3. The factors that are most irritating to consumers receiving unsolicited telemarketing calls

The technological principle behind the hardware device is fairly simple. It intercepts incoming calls before a ring signal is generated (or answered by an answering machine) and gives the caller a programmable call screening message, such as

> "You have reached a PreFone Filter™ and not an answering machine. Notice to all sales callers...place this name and number on your "do not call" list, at once. Fund raisers, please mail all of your requests. Now, personal and invited business callers press 5 on your touchtone phone. Rotary and pulse dial users please hold." (Note: Callers without tone phone equipment—about 30 percent of the population—can wait through two message cycles and the line opens up to their calls.)

This message is not heard by the person being called, and his or her telephone does not ring. Thus, without being disturbed, the call recipient has caused one or more of several things to happen:

1. Telephone sales representatives have heard the recording and disconnected. Under Public Law 102–243 they are legally required *not* to press 5 and be processed through to the consumer. (This law allows the consumer to notify all sales callers that the consumer

wants his or her name and number placed on the sellers' "do not call" list, thus prohibiting the caller from proceeding with further contact. This message constitutes legal notification under the law, and ignoring the callee's instruction, which is very unlikely, qualifies the caller as a harasser.)

2. Autodialer generated call equipment has "read" the recorded "something" and disconnected. Actually the computer auto-dialers sense that they are talking to an artificial voice and "hang up" before the telephone company can charge them with a phone call.

None of these activities involve the PreFone Filter™ user because the callee's telephone remains silent until 5 or another number has been pressed by the caller. Familiar frequent callers can press 5 after they hear the first ring (not heard by callee) without having to listen to the message. Special priority callers such as close family members, relatives, or good friends can be privately instructed to press 4 or 6 on their telephones and the phone will ring in a unique manner. When the PreFone Filter is switched off, the telephone responds as it would without the PreFone Filter present.

Three different versions of the product were developed: the Junk-Buster, the Standard, and the Deluxe. The JunkBuster model has a canned message, and the owner cannot record his or her own message. With the Standard model, the owner can either use the canned message or write and record his or her own. The Deluxe model allows the owner to not only record his or her own message but also to assign special rings to special people. Dr. Buchan thinks the Deluxe model should be priced at $149.50, the Standard model at $129.50, and the JunkBuster at $99.50.

The PreFone Filter™ does not solve all problems. The commercial caller can legally override the system with PreFone Filter™ users who possess call waiting systems. This is because the callee receives the usual signal that a call is "waiting." When this happens, the caller has been recognized without having to punch 5; in other words, he or she has gotten through. In this case the user will have to personally refuse conversation with the caller.

The PreFone Filter™ also stops all extension phones from ringing unless a device that causes them to ring is installed. This device (which costs about $15) can be programmed to ring extension phones selectively with specific numbers known to the caller.

According to its inventor, with the majority of telephone hardware situations, the PreFone Filter™ accomplishes many beneficial results for the users who wish to stop "junk" phone calls. These benefits include the following:

1. It provides a silent phone with no interruptions while the rejection of junk calls is being accomplished.
2. It requires no complex codes or numbers to issue and remember.
3. It allows regular calls to ring through at any time after the connection is made.
4. It does not require going to the phone and looking at or listening to anything.
5. It is compatible with all answering machines.
6. It receives both pulse and rotary dial telephone calls.
7. It takes only seconds to install.
8. It comes with a proven, legally worded message or can record the user's own unique message right from the telephone.
9. It is capable of assigning special rings to special people in the user's life.

Other Positive Business Uses of the PreFone Filter™

It is also possible that the PreFone Filter™ owner could use the device in positive ways. In screening junk calls, for example, the owner can use it to schedule a time when he or she will accept commercial calls. Such a time could easily be included in the message.

The device can also be used for a variety of tasks unrelated to the telephone. Among these is order-taking in drive-through restaurants. When drive-through fast-food restaurants take orders, the customer must be asked by a live order taker to give his or her order over an intercom. It is difficult for order takers to stay fresh and enthusiastic when this is done repetitiously, particularly when a special is being promoted. By installing a PreFone Filter™, activated by either the customer or by a restaurant employee, the asking for the order and/or promotion of a special can be done uniformly and enthusiastically throughout all of the restaurant's open hours.

Regardless of the model, installation of the PreFone Filter™ requires four steps: 1) unplug the telephone from the wall jack, 2) plug the unit into the wall jack, 3) plug the telephone into the unit, and 4) plug the power transformer into a 110V outlet and the PreFone Filter™. All connections are clearly marked. An illuminated on-off switch is on the front panel of the unit. In the "off" position, the unit is disabled and the telephone responds as it would with no PreFone Filter™ present.

In both the "on" and "off" modes, the unit is fully compatible with telephone answering machines. PreFone Filter™ comes with a professionally announced message; however, owners have the option of recording their own voice messages through the record/playback feature. Recommended scripts are provided. The unit is 100 percent guaranteed (obvious abuse excepted) for five years.

Future PIP, Inc. Products

The PreFone Filter™ is the first in a series of products that will use the preconditioning of inbound and outbound telephone signals to perform a variety of automatic functions and services.

Future products from PreFone Integrated Products include units designed for the following uses:

1. To monitor the consciousness and activity of the elderly. For example, a PreFone Filter™-type device with a strobe light preset to come on every two, four, six, or twelve hours. If persons at the site of the device do not touch the device and deactivate it, it will begin to ring the phone. If the phone is not answered after a set number of rings, preset numbers will be dialed. For example, nearest neighbor, relative 1, relative 2, and as a last resort, 911.
2. To significantly improve fire safety in occupied and unoccupied dwellings. Fire alarm devices remotely activate PreFone Filter™, which rings all phones in the dwelling. If the phone is not answered after a set number of rings, preset numbers will be dialed in a series. For example, nearest neighbor, relative 1, relative 2, and as a last resort, 911.
3. To provide for immediate-response emergency health care activity. PreFone Filter™ can be set to respond (without disturbing the callee) to a caller (son, daughter, etc.) who wants to know if the strobe light in an elderly or frail relative's dwelling has been touched at preappointed times. If not, the caller can activate the callee's phone, activating a series of calls for immediate help from neighbors or other people.
4. To perform other sensor-based notification and monitoring functions. For example, the strobe light can be set to come on (and if there is no response, the phone set to ring) at times when medicine should be taken, or at times when other activities should be started. It becomes, in effect, a programmable alarm clock.

Product Introduction Challenges

The development of the PreFone Filter™ was a difficult and expensive learning experience for Dr. Buchan. It required intensive research as well as effort to learn how to market a new product.

More money was expended in the development and initial marketing of the product than Dr. Buchan anticipated. He has already spent $300,000 of his own money for the product. Another difficulty was that because he did not have an established "storefront" business, he could not get permission to take orders with Visa or other credit cards unless he first put $100,000 on deposit in the bank sponsoring the credit card.

Dr. Buchan also had problems with the distribution network. He found that suppliers of parts for his early production models would not issue credit. In addition, they required a minimum order of at least 1000 units at $75 per unit for a bottom-of-the-line Junk-Buster, $95 for the Standard, and $115 for the Deluxe. These costs are estimated to fall to $55, $80, and $100 respectively once the unit is put into quantity production, and ultimately to the $35 to $50 range.

One major concern of many new inventors was not a problem for this inventor. Because he had prior experience with inventions, he was able to quickly do the paperwork needed to receive patents. Hardware patents and software copyrights are pending. Large blocks of the circuitry are applicable to later products, reducing design-to-market time and costs. He also quickly "locked up" for future use the telephone number 1-800-No2JUNK, or 1-800-662-5865.

Initial Marketing Concepts

Dr. Buchan had little marketing knowledge and experience. Several people offered to license and market the product for him, doing business as PreFone Integrated Products Inc. (PIP). Among these were Burnell Henshaw and Carole Seeby[7],—freelance direct marketing consultants who proposed to license and market the PreFone Filter™ and other products designed by Dr. Buchan. The first step in their recommendation was a test marketing program for the Pre-Fone Filter™. Two guiding principles drove the development of this program:

1. Need for a test of the market at minimum costs while yielding maximum "readability of results"
2. Need for a phased approach permitting decisions at critical points, thereby minimizing risk and investment

The following is an outline of their proposal.

A test "go-for-the-order" newspaper advertisement would be run in the Southwestern Edition of *The Wall Street Journal*. Henshaw and Seeby felt strongly that all the product and other information necessary for the buyer to make a decision could be included in such an ad.

This ad would reach approximately 200,000 readers, and cost approximately $3000 to place (about 1.5 cents per reader) plus creative

---

[7]These names have been disguised at the request of the participants.

and production costs. Creative costs would be from $5,000 to $10,000, and production costs would be approximately $750. Thus, the cost to produce and place the ad was estimated to be a minimum of approximately $9,000 and a maximum of approximately $14,000. Such a test should determine three things: 1) is there a market for the PreFone Filter™? 2) at which test price does the product sell the most profitably? and 3) who is the best prospect for the product? (At this point in time, no mass production has been accomplished; production would, of course, have to be in place to supply orders from the test.)

The test advertisement was to be three newspaper columns wide and 8.5 inches high—enough space to present the product graphically, tell the sales story, and aggressively ask for orders.

Orders were to be placed by telephone, toll-free, and taken on credit cards only. An inbound telemarketing organization would handle order taking, with ordering available 24 hours a day, 7 days a week. The buyer was to be asked to pay handling and postage of approximately $5. Order-processing costs were estimated to be a net additional cost to the product of approximately $5. Orders would be transferred to Henshaw and Seeby and Associates, who would fulfill them.

Henshaw and Seeby proposed that Dr. Buchan advance them the sum necessary to finance the test, and possibly a revision of it to improve results. This would permit Henshaw and Seeby to contract for the services necessary to conduct the test. They would then coordinate all the activities required to get orders for the product and ensure they were properly shipped. Henshaw and Seeby offered to waive their consulting fees for these preliminary activities in exchange for later equity participation in a marketing company to be organized upon completion and success of the test marketing plan.

PIP, Inc., was to be responsible for producing the product. After the test, all projected costs and profit prospects would be considered and a decision made on whether to roll out the product or try another approach. A positive test in most cases of this sort would be the achievement of an advertising/sales ratio in the range of 25 to 30 percent. For example, if the response at a price of $139 is 80 units, sales will be $11,120, which when divided into $3000 (ad costs) results in an advertising/sales ratio of 26.5 percent. In most cases such results would be adequate to support a viable business.

Burnell Henshaw and Carole Seeby offered to organize a marketing company called BHS (Buchan, Henshaw, and Seeby), with Burnell Henshaw as Chief Executive Officer and Carole Seeby as President. Robert Buchan was to receive a royalty of $1 per unit or 2 percent of manufacturing costs, whichever was higher, in addition to his equity participation.

Dr. Buchan was to remain responsible for maintaining patent protection by challenging the legitimacy of similar products. (Patents are good only until someone else finds a way around them).

At the time of Henshaw and Seeby's proposal, the product was not ready for production because the circuitry in the device needed to be field tested and refined before being fully implemented. As a result, Dr. Buchan thought an aggressive selling program at this time was premature. For this reason, and also because he was still undecided as to the best organization for development and marketing of the product, Dr. Buchan decided against the Henshaw and Seeby test marketing proposal.

He continued moving ahead on his own, however, and during this process contacted a major direct marketing advertising agency for assistance in developing a direct-response marketing plan and program. This turned out to be a very unsatisfactory experience. Dr. Buchan felt that the agency's personnel were not interested in what he knew about the market for the PreFone Filter™. As a result, he believed that they were making some very naive recommendations that were going to cost him much money unnecessarily.

For this reason, and also because he wanted to sell the unit slowly at first until it had been field tested, Dr. Buchan decided, for the time being, to market the product himself by generating leads with public relations announcement stories about the product in newspapers and magazines—which could be had for nothing when reporters and editors could be interested in the product enough to write a story—and converting them with a direct mail package.

Accordingly, he laid out a product brochure on his home computer, developed a sales letter, and mounted a sustained program of contacting various media for the purpose of getting stories written about the product. This strategy produced inquiries from potential customers, who were sent the brochure and sales letter. The conversion rate on these was satisfactory but not outstanding; however, the process was putting units to actual use in normal consumer situations. It also turned up an unexpected source of inquiries and sales: "word-of-ear" began generating both inquiries and sales, as persons who heard the device on phones they were calling became interested in the product.

Buoyed by these results, Dr. Buchan then decided to test mail his brochure and sales letter (see Exhibit 10-1) to a list of 5000 persons known to have complained about junk phone calls. This mailing offered to sell the Deluxe version of the PreFone Filter™ device for $158.50. The test results were poor, however, suggesting that a one-

Exhibit 10-1   Cover Letter for PreFone Filter™ Mail Conversion Package

Dear Mr(s). Prospect:

At last, there is a **silent, guaranteed solution** to those aggravating junk call interruptions of quality time at home and valuable time at work!

Before your telephone rings, the legally exact wording required to **stop all sales solicitors** is clearly announced, in your voice or ours, thereby making it a Federal offense for them to disturb you. Regular, desirable callers can gain instant access to your line, thus by-passing the screening message.

It works! Not one of our customers has reported receiving a **single** unsolicited sales call or fund raising request in over a year of generalized use!

The guaranteed performance of one of our three models will fully meet your expectations of finally achieving personal telephone privacy. **Risk nothing** with our 30 day trial, no-questions-asked, money-back offer.

The *JunkBuster*™ Model at $99.50, invokes the precise rejection words in our clear preprogrammed human voice. Simply plug it in and enjoy the end of unwanted telephone disruptions. A $7.95 per month check-o-matic lease is available to qualified customers.

The *PreFone Filter*™ Model at $129.50, provides you with the ability to deliver your own unique custom screening message. You record your voice right from your telephone as many times and ways as you wish. No mikes, no tapes, no hassle! Suggestions for custom messages are provided. Qualified customers may also pay on a check-o-matic lease basis for this as well as the *Deluxe* Model, below.

The *PreFone Filter*™ Deluxe Model at $149.95, adds breakthrough technology to the standard model, above, to allow you to assign **special distinctive sounding ring signals** to special people or groups. Let calls from loved ones and special friends be recognized at once! Give teenage callers their special sounding ring! The possibilities are endless and limited only by your imagination!

All three models employ up-to-the-minute, computer based, advanced electronic circuitry. Flawless performance is fully warranted. We are an American company carefully selecting American made components, with all assembly, packaging and distribution functions originating here in the Mid-West U.S.A.

Check our comparative costs of inferior alternatives!
Check out our 100 percent Rebate Plan...a enational offer!
Check out the rock-solid warranty!

Don't tolerate these privacy invasions another day! Send your order in the postage-free envelope today and permanent relief from junk call misery will be on its way!

The PreFone Filter™ Company.

step direct marketing mail program would be unprofitable. Nevertheless, the test did reveal some useful information. For example, it was quite clear that there was substantial price resistance at $158.50. This led Dr. Buchan to conclude that $99.50, $129.50, and $149.50 were probably his best prices.

Dr. Buchan is now convinced that the device has been perfected, and he is ready to consider an aggressive move into the marketplace. He is, however, still undecided as to what he should do and how he should do it. His only strong opinion is that he would much prefer to be involved in the manufacturing and development side of the product and let someone else sell it.

Questions

1. Is there a market or markets for the PreFone Filter™?
2. What are some alternative ways to sell this product? What is the best way to introduce—initially sell—the product?
3. How should Dr. Buchan organize to produce and market the product? For example, a production and a marketing company? Production only with sales and marketing licensed to someone else?
4. How should Dr. Buchan finance the production and introduction of his new product?
5. How valid is the pricing approach suggested in the case? Can the PreFone Filter™ device be sold profitably at the prices Dr. Buchan believes should be used? Why or why not?
6. What are the objections to buying the product, besides price, that consumers are likely to raise? Can these be overcome?
7. What are the merits of the "test direct marketing" program suggested by Henshaw and Seeby? Does it make sense? What about the test run by Dr. Buchan?
8. What are some of the positioning concepts (big ideas/copy platforms) that might be used as the cutting edge of whatever advertising or other promotional programs that are used?
9. Does Dr. Buchan need to conduct further consumer research?
10. What do you think Dr. Buchan should do?

The authors wish to gratefully acknowledge a contributing author, Nabil Hassan, Professor, Wright State University.

Case 11

Baby Blankets by Mail
Creating a Complete Direct Marketing Strategy

If you take a useful article of merchandise, put an advertising message on it, and distribute it, you have specialty advertising. Calendars are probably the best-known ad specialty item, but imprinted pens, key chains, coffee mugs, articles of clothing, and thousands of other items also qualify. Business gifts, which are used primarily for goodwill and to say "Thank You!" are also included under the advertising specialty umbrella. Advertising specialties is the business of the S.E. Bennett company, a Cleveland, Ohio, firm owned by Tom and Jackie Ullmo.

The S.E. Bennett company had eight employees, including the Ullmos. Two employees were salespeople who called on accounts located primarily in Michigan, Illinois, Ohio, and New York; two employees handled client communications related to order fulfillment; and two worked in the Cleveland offices. Tom and Jackie shared management responsibilities: Tom placed his emphasis on product search and selection and on generating ideas for improving sales, and Jackie spent most of her time directing the day-to-day operations of the company.

The company had a large client base that included several Fortune 500 companies. Sales were approximately $3 million and growing at about 5 percent per year. The company's net profit after taxes was comparable to similar firms. The firm's assets totaled approximately $400,000. Its debt was zero.

Direct Marketing Opportunity Emerges

The Ullmos had been utilizing direct-response techniques to generate and qualify leads and were aware of several major direct-response marketing success stories. As a result, they had been considering adding a direct mail marketing operation to their marketing program for some time but had never found a product that seemed appropriate. Then, a product came to their attention that looked viable. The product was a unique baby blanket sold by one of their advertising specialty product suppliers. Almost simultaneously, First Markets, a direct mail co-op that appeared to be an ideal medium in which to offer the blanket, came to their attention. Thinking that they had discovered both a good direct mail product and an excellent vehicle for reaching its market, the Ullmos were poised to put together a program to sell the blanket by mail. But before finalizing their decision to offer the baby blanket through the direct mail channel, the

Ullmos decided to discuss their plans with Tom Wiseman, a long-time friend who also happened to be a direct-response marketing consultant.

Over dinner with Wiseman, the Ullmos outlined their thoughts and tentative plans in some detail. Their plan included installing a toll-free 800 number and taking both mail and phone orders for the blankets at their Cleveland offices. These, in turn, would be forwarded to the supplier for fulfillment. Wiseman and the Ullmos also held a wide-ranging discussion on what the requirements for successfully selling the blanket by mail would be. Wiseman was very firm in his belief that direct mail success with the blanket would result only if the blanket was a good fit with the direct-response channel.

Good Direct-Response Products

Wiseman stressed that in order for the blanket to sell well in the direct response channel, it would probably have to possess a good measure of six characteristics usually found in successful direct-response products. These were universal appeal, unusual features, not readily available, proper price and profit margins, a dream or story element, and continuing sales potential.

By universal appeal, Tom meant that the baby blanket should appeal to virtually every member on the mailing list or database segment that was mailed, or to the entire readership of any publication in which direct-response ads would appear.

Tom also stressed that there should be some unusual feature or features in the basic product. In other words, the baby blanket should be unique in some way. In the direct marketing channel, skillful copy and graphics can highlight unusual features of the product and build desire for it. Thus, even if the baby blanket were an ordinary or slow-moving product when sold in retail stores, it might be made to come alive if offered in the direct response channel—assuming the existence of one or more unusual features.

Tom also pointed out that the lack of ready availability is one of the main things a successful direct marketing offer has going for it. Accordingly, it should not be easy for prospective buyers to find the same baby blanket in stores, or at least not to find it offered in stores at the S.E. Bennett price or perhaps not offered with S.E. Bennett's particular package of offer elements.

Proper price and profit margins, with reasonable packaging and shipping costs, was another criterion Wiseman felt the baby blanket should have. He noted that the price requirement in the direct-response channel is usually three times cost for one-step, go-for-the-order mail order programs and twice the cost for catalog sales. (This is an average that comes from the experience of thousands of successful mail order marketers.) But according to Tom, perhaps the most important pricing issue of all was making sure that the price of the baby blanket would "feel" right to the audience. In his words, "you don't sell $3 ties to $200,000-a-year executives. The price wouldn't feel right to them."

Another attribute of good direct mail products is continuing sales potential. In other words, can the buyers of the blanket be sold more of the product, or be sold something else? If so, this will mean later sales at much lower cost per order than that of the first sale, and, therefore, much more profitable future direct marketing to blanket buyers.

Finally, in Tom Wiseman's view, the presence of a dream or story element would add considerably to the direct mail channel viability of the baby blanket. His point was that if the blanket could be presented as offering a quick fix, a gain without much pain—a dream, if you will, or if there was an intriguing story associated with it, involving either the product or its discoverer or designer, this might be just the thing to put the blanket over the top in the direct mail channel.

The Direct-Response Tripod

Wiseman was also quite emphatic in his view that the direct marketing program for the blanket should be based on a clear understanding of what he termed the "direct response tripod." This is a concept that emphasizes and ties together three specific and major direct marketing decisions that must be carefully made. These are the list choice, the offer choice, and the positioning or copy platform choice. Direct marketing failure can usually be traced to ineffectiveness in one of these areas. Some of Wiseman's specific advice on these issues is outlined below.

Direct Mail Lists

Wiseman said that a list would likely be a good one for the baby blanket only if everyone on it could reasonably be assumed to be a prospect for the blanket. Otherwise, he said, the economics usually don't work out. He also noted that, in direct marketing, the list is the market. Thus, whatever program was put together for the baby blanket should be faithful to the specific needs and aspirations of persons on the target list or to specific segments within it, and to no one else. Furthermore, for purposes of program development, all buyers other than those on the list being targeted should, for program purposes, be disregarded. In sum, S.E. Bennett should make a good offer designed and positioned specifically for a particular list.

Direct Mail Offers

Tom described a good offer as one that melts away prospect resistance and obtains the order or the lead immediately. In the baby blanket case, he said that "offer" should be taken to mean the blanket plus any or all of the following: time limits for buyer acceptance, guarantees, payment terms, delivery terms, the price, return privileges, and premiums for ordering now or for ordering at all. In total, the S.E. Bennett offer would be the price and everything else the buyer would be asked to give to S.E. Bennett in exchange for the blanket and everything else the S.E. Bennett Company would be committing to give to the buyer. Offers for the blanket could be structured in an enormous variety of ways, with each one offering significantly different potential sales results. Accordingly, a large amount of creative effort could and probably should go into structuring whatever offer S.E. Bennett decided to make.

Positioning the Direct Mail Offer

Wiseman explained that positioning is being done when the seller decides what will be presented as the basic benefit bundle, or as the "big story" about the product. Experienced direct marketers have found that a mail program works best when it is built around one, and only one, major concept. In the baby blanket case, the big story might be, for example, enhanced baby comfort, or perhaps, creating a permanent reminder of a period in a child's life. Whatever story is chosen, all sales literature should reflect it. The term "literature" should be understood to include sales letters, brochures, order forms, and even telephone sales scripts, if the telephone is part of the program's media mix.

Direct Marketing Formats

According to Tom Wiseman, once the list, offer, and positioning issues concerning the baby blanket were thoroughly resolved, the strategy would have a solid conceptual foundation, and S.E. Bennett would be ready to develop marketing materials and other elements of the program. This, he said, would require selection of a presentation vehicle from among the three basic direct mail formats: the classic package, the self-mailer, and the catalog.

The classic package is a mailing that includes an outside envelope, a cover letter, a brochure, an order form, a lift device or premium of some sort, and a response device. The function of the outside envelope is to get itself opened. That is why there is often a teaser on the envelope. The function of the brochure is to "show and tell" or explain the product or service. The function of the cover letter is to explain and sell (motivate the prospect to buy) the offer (of product, at current price, with current premium, and so on) that is being made. The order form is the closing device. The function of the lift device or premium (which can be a discount, an additional product, or other incentive) is to induce a decision now, and overcome procrastination, which is the death knell of direct marketers. In Wiseman's view, all of the functions performed by elements of the classic package would have to be performed in some way in the blanket mail package, whatever its format. Accordingly, if, for example, a self-mailer were selected as the presentation vehicle for the blanket, it would need to contain elements designed to get itself opened, show and tell the product, explain and sell the offer, ask for the order, and overcome buyer procrastination.

Finally, according to Tom Wiseman, the direct marketing media that might be considered for the blanket should not be limited to the mail. He mentioned that the telephone, newspapers, magazines, and take-ones, to name just a few of many direct marketing media, were also options that might have merit. He also noted that the direct-response marketing concept embraces programs all the way from those used to generate leads for a product or service to programs that ask for customer commitment to buy. His larger point was that the Ullmos might want to consider using direct marketing tools for only one step of the sales cycle, such as for generating or for qualifying sales leads or for providing prospects with detailed information about the blanket; the task of actually closing the sale could be left to higher-impact, and higher-cost, personal or telephone selling.

The "Lullabye Crib Blanket" and Its Supplier

The blanket the Ullmos wanted to sell was called the Faribo "Lullabye Crib Blanket." It was being produced by the Faribault Woolen Mill Company, a 125 year-old, family-owned specialty blanket manufacturer located on the banks of the Cannon River in Faribault, Minnesota.

Faribault described the Lullaby Crib Blanket as "washable/dryable (without fear of shrinkage), permanently mothproofed (guaranteed), 60 percent wool and 40 percent acrylic, 45 inches by 55 inches in size, and trimmed with an elegant satin binding on all four sides." The fibers blended together in a unique thermal weave designed to provide light-weight warmth. The wool provided warmth and durability, and the acrylic added luxurious texture and easy care.

Faribault monogrammed each blanket, in either script or block style, with the baby's first name or initials and date of birth. No other monogramming was permitted. Buyers could choose either a white, blue, or pink blanket and select either navy, light blue, white, burgundy, pink, or metallic gold thread for the monogram. The monogram was approximately 2 inches high and tastefully positioned in the corner of the blanket.

Faribault had a reputation for producing very high-quality blankets. The company had established this reputation by selling only high-quality blankets and by offering each buyer the following written "Endless Guarantee":

> If at any time during normal use, and following Faribo's recommended care instructions, your blanket does not live up to the superb tradition of Faribo workmanship and materials, return it to the store where it was purchased or send written notification of the failure to Faribo Blankets, P.O. Box 369, Faribault, Minnesota 55021. Please advise product name, size, color, and source from whom the blanket was purchased. Instructions regarding the return and replacement of the defective blanket will follow.

Faribault already had in place a "Warm Regards" certificate program which the Ullmos could use as it was, or improve on, if need be. This involved the buyer ordering a gift certificate for the Lullabye Crib Blanket, rather than the blanket itself.

The Warm Regards certificate package contained four pieces. The first was an outer envelope on which the gift-giver could write the recipient's name. This envelope contained a second envelope that contained a piece designed to communicate "best wishes" to the new arrival. Inside this piece was a tastefully done third piece that was used to 1) "sell" the blanket to the certificate recipient, 2) show a picture of blankets in all three color options, 3) show the six different thread color selections, and 4) illustrate the block and script style lettering options. The fourth piece was a self-addressed and postage-paid redemption card that the recipient used to indicate the color, script, and information choices. This was returned to Faribault, who then monogrammed the blanket in the selected thread color and shipped it to the certificate recipient in a special gift box. The recipient was advised to allow three to four weeks for delivery. Each certificate was numbered for tracking purposes.

Summary of Discussions with Mothers and Others

Preliminary discussions by the Ullmos with mothers and others who were thought to be prospects for the blanket revealed a variety of perspectives on the blanket's value and potential uses. Mothers' comments included the following: "It looks like good quality." "I'd be concerned about the wool scratching the baby." "I'd be interested at $30 to $40." "It looks like something I'd want to keep." "The inscriptions are very nice. I'd give one to a friend." "I think new mothers are likely to know someone who is having a baby." "New mothers are more likely than others to be giving a baby shower, or know someone who is giving a baby shower." "This is something a mother might like to get as the honoree at a baby shower."

Other comments the Ullmos received contained suggestions: "Mothers won't buy them after the baby is born." "They're full-up with this type of merchandise by the time the baby comes, and have too many other things on their mind." "This product will sell better to Grandmas, friends, etc., as a gift, than directly to mothers." "Might want to sell it through *Rotary Magazine* to affluent grandfathers and through a comparable women's magazine to grandmothers." "How about selling the blanket without the monogramming?" "How about using a package of games to be played at baby showers as a premium?" "How about a 'How to Do a Baby Shower' booklet as a premium?" "How about giving a separate plaque with baby's name, birth date, etc., as a premium for buying the blanket?" "Could the blankets be monogrammed with something other than baby's name, birth date, etc.—for example, teddy bears?"

Ready Availability of Testimonials

The S.E. Bennett Company gave sample blankets to several clients as Christmas gifts and received a variety of laudatory comments about them. Here's a sample:

1. The Faribo "Lullabye Crib Blanket" is warm and doesn't ravel with wear. The initials and date of birth mean we will keep the blanket forever. We highly recommend this blanket. (Mrs. Kathy Miller)
2. When Jason was born, we received many, many gifts. The most practical gift was a Faribo "Lullabye Crib Blanket." We have been stopped in stores by people who want to know where they can buy one. Jason still will not go to sleep without "his" blanket with "his" name on it. (Mrs. Sara Kluck)
3. When my twins Erin and Randi were born, it was a momentous occasion. The best gifts we received were Faribo blankets for both girls with their initials on each blanket. It is a warm and cuddly blanket that each girl loves. Even though people can't tell the difference between the girls, the girls know "their" blankets. (Mrs. Natalie Vinocur)
4. The blanket that we received when Sally was born is truly unique and outstanding. The construction is first class. The monogramming of the baby's name and birth date means we will treasure the blanket always. (Mrs. Elaine Browning)

Direct Product Costs and Anticipated Price

S.E. Bennett's cost was $25 for each blanket, which included the cost of sewn-in inscriptions of names and birth dates, as well as the cost of the packaging and shipment of blankets to individual direct mail buyers. The range of prices that comparable blankets were selling for in retail stores was $40 to $50, but these prices did not include the monogramming and special gift box offered with the Lullabye Crib Blanket.

The First Markets Co-op

The Ullmos were excited about using a direct mail co-op called First Markets in their first direct marketing test. First Markets was selling exclusive distribution of direct marketing materials to expectant and new mothers. The company delivered "kits" or boxes containing a large, loose variety of noncompeting printed offers and product samples in plastic bags to hospitals across the nation. The hospitals routinely distributed the kits to their patients. Two different kits were distributed. One was an expectant parents' kit; the other was a new parents' kit. The "new parent" kits came in bags that were blue or pink depending on whether the child was a boy or girl.

The following list of contents was found in one delivery of both types of kits:

- Product samples of the following:
    Baby Magic Baby Bath
    Baby Magic Baby Lotion
    Parke-Davis Tucks Pads
    Baby Care Magazine
    Pampers Disposable Diapers
- A gift certificate for *Baby Care Magazine*
- Flyers or brochures on the following:
    Sony HandyCam Camcorders
    Speas Farm Apple Juice
    Luvs Baby Club
    Sears Portrait Studio
    Nip-E-Z (never boil a nipple again)
    Even Flo disposable bottles
    A and D Ointment (for baby rash)
    Baby Booties
    Parents Magazine
    Kodak Film
    JC Penney portrait specials
    Mylicon Drops (a colic reliever) and coupons from Johnson & Johnson/Merck

Ivory Snow (with coupons)
Gerber baby formula (with coupon)
Beech-Nut Stages (Baby Foods)
Kelloggs Special K
Toys "R" Us (including coupons)
Wash-a-bye Baby Wipes (including coupons)
First Six Month Insurance (from First Markets, Inc.)
Dr. Seuss books from Grolier
Disney Books (book club)
Children's Tylenol (contained along with coupons in information pamphlet in both English and Spanish)
Tylenol Gelcaps (pamphlet in both English and Spanish)
Aerre Air Freshener for nurseries
Charmin tissue (coupons in a pamphlet on hemorrhoids)
- A catalog from Fisher Price (infant product guide)

Distribution of the Expectant Parents' Kit

First Markets' Expectant Parents' Kit was delivered annually through Lamaze educators to approximately 1.9 million expectant couples as a classroom supplement in childbirth education classes. These kits were received by expectant parents during the seventh month of pregnancy. A new supply of kits was distributed to hospitals quarterly—giving marketers four different opportunities to insert an offer in them. They were distributed by hospitals to new parents. Demographics of the recipients of these kits are shown in Table 11-1.

Table 11-1 Demographics of Expectant Parent Kit Recipients

Age of Parents	Percent of Mothers	Percent of Fathers
<20	6.2	2.8
21–25	31.1	22.0
26–29	35.2	28.2
30–35	23.6	33.6
36–40	3.6	10.1
>40	0.0	3.3

Highest Education in Household (Percent)		Average Yearly Household Income	Percent
Attended high school	1.7	<$10M	7.9
High school graduate	13.8	10.1–20M	21.9
Attended college	24.1	20.1–30M	27.1
College graduate	30.5	30.1–40M	21.9
Post graduate	9.0	40.1–50M	11.5
Post graduate degree	20.9	>50M	9.7

Distribution of the New Parents' Kit

First Markets' New Parents' Sampler was being delivered nationwide to approximately 3.5 million mothers a year. These packages were distributed to hospitals monthly and ultimate delivery to mothers was guaranteed. To assure this, a CPA firm had been retained by First Markets to perform periodic audits. Hospital staff nurses gave these kits to mothers 24 hours after a baby's birth. First Markets claimed that nine of every ten hospital births triggered the delivery of a new parents' kit.

The minimum test quantity of either of the First Markets kits was 50,000. First Markets' charges were based on size, weight, and distribution volume. The Ullmos estimated that it would cost S.E. Bennett $2500 to include one test piece in a test kit going to 50,000 mothers or couples—assuming the test pieces were no larger or heavier than an 8½-by-11-inch sheet of paper. A test distribution of 100,000 could be run for $4000. Beyond 100,000, discounts for volume were minimal. These costs would be in addition to any other charges S.E. Bennett incurred in the preparation of the test package such as photography, printing, and the like.

First Markets supplied all users of the co-op with the names of all new and expectant mothers who received a kit containing their offers. First Markets also supplied their clients with the names of kit recipients who returned the coded business reply card that was included in every expectant parents' kit. This card asked for the recipient's location, the number of children in the family and their ages, and the like. The business reply card information and the lists of names supplied by First Markets allowed the kit users to do follow-up research to determine why their offers were successful or unsuccessful with various types of people and to learn how to revise their pieces for better results the next time they were included in a First Markets kit.

Questions

1. Is it strategically sound for S.E. Bennett to pursue growth by entering the direct marketing business?
2. What are the foundations on which a successful direct mail marketing program for the baby blanket, if undertaken by the Ullmos, will rest?
3. Does the Faribo "Lullabye Baby Blanket" have the attributes of a good direct response product?
4. Evaluate the "First Markets" co-op lists as direct mail lists and decide the Ullmos' probable success if these lists are chosen as the initial promotional channels for the Faribo "Lullabye Baby Blanket."

5. Identify several viable "positioning" concepts for use with the "Lul-labye Baby Blanket," and recommend one of these as your choice for the copy platform in the initial Faribo "Lullabye Baby Blan-ket" direct marketing program.
6. Create an offer that will melt away customer resistance and sell the "Lullabye Baby Blanket" to the market of your choice.
7. Prepare a total marketing plan for launching the baby blanket. Include a budget.

The authors wish to gratefully acknowledge a contributing author, Nabil Hassan, Professor, Wright State University.

Case 12 Allwood Chef, Inc.
Program Development for a New Consumer Product

Ed Phillips, a small welding shop operator in Southern Illinois, was stricken with a rare disease. After several years and all of Ed's savings, doctors had diagnosed his problem, which, it turned out, was potentially curable, though it left Ed in a weakened condition.

No longer able to do heavy work, Ed, a proud man, began doing any kind of light work he could find to earn a living and pay for his continuing medical treatments. While working in a pizza parlor in 1989, Ed suddenly hit on the idea of catering company picnics and other social events where large numbers of people were gathered for meals cooked on site. Ed's idea quickly turned into a reality and after six months Ed's Catering Service became a thriving business. As it grew, Ed toyed with several different cooking methods and cooker concepts with the goal of finding a way to cook enough meat to serve up to 600 people at one time and still get a distinctive, flavorful result.

One day while discussing a catering job with a company that produced household fuel oil tanks, an idea occurred to Ed. A fuel oil tank just might be configured in some way to produce the result he wanted. After considerable thought, Ed decided that he must separate the fire from the food in such a way that the grease would not drop onto the fire. Ed designed a "separator" (technically a "baffle") that he placed one-third of the way down into the fuel tank. The baffle permitted the fire to burn in the upper third of the fuel tank, and allowed the heat and smoke to circulate down into the lower two-thirds of the tank where the meat was cooked. The smoke would escape through an exhaust at the bottom end of the tank.

After experimenting with various ways of dampering the contraption, lowering and raising the height of the baffle, trying several exhaust locations, and developing various sizes and types of access doors, Ed developed a primitive version of his cooker. To facilitate movement of the cooker, Ed placed it on wheels.

Because one of his cookers could serve up to 100 people, Ed decided to construct six of them so that he could serve up to 600 people at one time. Never satisfied, Ed decided to combine the six cookers into one giant cooker that could be towed to a site and used to cook for any size group. He proceeded by stringing three of the tanks end to end and then placing the two strings side by side on a specially built trailer. By extending the proportionality derived from his one-fuel-tank cooker to an end-wise combination of three fuel tanks, he was able to get the same taste and flavor as before. Ed immediately dubbed the new cooker the "Gourmet Cooker."

Ed thought he might have something that was patentable, and to his surprise, he did. He proceeded to obtain a patent.

Ed attempted to sell a license on his patented process to others, but there were no takers. He learned later that several restaurants were using his cooker idea in some of their units. After several caustic confrontations with the owners and managers of these restaurants, Ed sued one of them for infringing on his patent and won. Unfortunately for Ed, however, although the restaurants stopped using Ed's idea (presumably because of his suit), they did not show much interest in making a deal with Ed for rights to use his new gourmet cooking concept.

Ed's patent was somewhat strange in that it patented a result—the double-spiral, heated gas flow—not the cooker itself. Thus, the patent precluded any charcoal burner makers from producing a cooker that used his heat movement process unless they paid Ed a royalty. None of them wanted it, however, until reports began to circulate that a chemical produced when grease dropped from cooking meat onto hot charcoal was potentially carcinogenic. This report made Ed feel he really did have a good idea because his cooker placed the fire above the meat where grease could not drop on the fire. Further, his cooker could be fired with wood as well as charcoal. With this thought, Ed Phillips proceeded to design a backyard-size "Gourmet Cooker."

The model he constructed was 36 inches long, 14 inches wide, and 20 inches deep. Because he couldn't buy ready-made fuel tanks for a cooker this size, he proceeded to develop primitive presses and molds to make his model in quantity. Made of steel and weighing over 100 pounds, Ed's cooker cost over $75 to build, assuming a production rate of about 20 cookers per day. Because Ed believed he would have no trouble selling a product such as his cooker with so many positive features, he proceeded to produce over 200 units. At a price of $120, Ed succeeded in selling a few units; however, the going was rough. In fact, two years passed before he was able to sell his total inventory of 200 backyard units, most of which he sold at his catering jobs where people saw how they worked. Frustrated, Ed could not understand why his cookers were not selling.

Everyone who owned a Gourmet Cooker raved about it! But orders were not coming in. His dealers, about 20 small retailers in Southern Indiana and Illinois, were very enthusiastic about his cookers; however, they were not moving them. The reason, presumably, was the price.

During this period, several charcoal cooker makers approached Ed with offers to buy his operation; however, the money they offered was trivial. None was willing to give Ed a reasonable per-unit royalty or minimum annual guarantee. Ed strongly suspected that all they wanted to do was "cubbyhole" his idea until his patent expired.

Not until five years after getting his patent, did Ed see any real hope of making money on his idea. While vacationing at a friend's home, Alfred Wisdom, a marketing professor at a nearby university, happened to notice with particular interest a backyard cooker which his friend had purchased from Phillips. Noticing the strange cooker, Wisdom asked his friend how the cooker functioned and what circumstances led him to purchase it. Although Professor Wisdom found his friend's story about the cooker interesting, he thought little more about it until about a month later. While having lunch with Larry Savage, an executive at Woodworks, Inc., a direct response firm for whom he was doing some consulting work, Wisdom mentioned the cooker as a possible novelty item in which the firm might be interested. His description of this unique cooker (see Exhibit 12-1) piqued Mr. Savage's interest. As a result, Professor Wisdom was invited to enter into exploratory discussions with the company's president and production manager concerning the advisability of adding such a product to the firm's line of woodworking equipment and supplies.

John Mercer, the company president, was moderately enthusiastic about the idea but felt that his company should explore the opportunity further. Mercer asked Wisdom to visit Ed Phillips and to enter into negotiations with him about the possibility of Woodworks, Inc., buying a license to market Phillips's patented product.

Wisdom telephoned Phillips and found that, indeed, he was looking for someone to market his cooker. However, Phillips was very evasive in answering most of Wisdom's other questions. To Wisdom it was apparent that Phillips feared Woodworks, Inc., was just another company that wanted to buy his patent for "pennies," only to market the cooker after the patent had expired.

One day while talking with several local people who knew Professor Wisdom, Phillips began to feel that Wisdom was a trustworthy person. After considerable thought, Phillips called Wisdom and agreed to bring his cooker to the company's headquarters to demonstrate how it worked. After explaining the merits of his unique cooking process, Phillips sat down with company management to discuss a possible licensing agreement.

Exhibit 12-1   Product Description and Comments

The Gourmet Cooker (The GC) is a truly multipurpose food preparation product. Either charcoal or wood may be used in it to generate cooking heat. Food may be cooked in it directly over charcoal or cooked indirectly with either charcoal or wood. It can be used to cook or smoke food or to do both simultaneously. It will cook meat, poultry, fish, and vegetables as well as bake bread. It can be used to dry fruit such as apples, apricots, and prunes. A variety of foods can be prepared on it at one time.

The GC's unique double spiral heat flow produces even heat throughout its cooking/smoking chamber. As a consequence, food is evenly cooked without being turned or "rotisseried." Also, because the GC's firebox is not under the food, flame-ups produced when grease hits charcoal are eliminated.

The GC gives flavor options equal to the variety of woods found in nature. Hickory wood imparts the delightful and traditional hickory flavor to whatever is being cooked. Sassafras and maple produce equally unique and delightful, flavorful taste treats.

Large hams, roasts, chickens, and the like can be cooked and/or smoked to perfection and then frozen until needed. At serving time, users need only microwave, oven heat, or pan heat the foods, or some meats like ham and chicken are also good served cold.

Unlike other cookers, particularly those that use gas as well as charcoal, the GC does not consume a nonrenewable natural resource. Wood is available virtually everywhere and is easily replenished. Also, it is not always necessary to burn new wood to get the wood-smoked flavors, as these can be obtained to some extent by burning available sawdust from various tree varieties on charcoal.

The sight and aroma of burning wood as it cooks food bring the GC user into much closer contact with nature. This product is not for those who take a rush-hour view of dining. It slows the user down and allows him or her to relax and do things the way our ancestors did them and to enjoy the process the way they did.

The GC is for those who appreciate good food, who take pride in preparing food to flavor perfection, and who find an escape from the hustle, rush, and bustle of modern life in their preparation of nutritious, natural, and naturally-flavored foods.

Alfred Wisdom

Ed was quite explicit in stating that unless he could earn at least $100,000 per year, he would not be interested in selling his patent rights. (He intimated, however, that his figure was somewhat negotiable.) Also, Ed wanted Woodworks, Inc., to satisfy a $3,000 loan he had incurred to make his primitive production equipment. Finally, Phillips wanted to continue to produce his cooker until his royalty payments exceeded what he was currently making on the units he was selling. Woodworks, Inc., executives believed Phillips's demand posed a set of serious problems for them. They also did not know how easy it might be for another company to find a way around his patent and imitate his cooker.

After considerable discussion of these and other issues with his chief executives, Mercer asked Professor Wisdom to outline a tentative offer to Phillips. However, while Professor Wisdom was preparing this document, Woodworks, Inc., executives were having second thoughts. They concluded that at the present time it was not wise to depart from their rapidly growing woodworking lines. Thus, no offer was made to Phillips.

Having learned of Woodworks' decision, Professor Wisdom began to entertain thoughts of marketing Phillips's cooker himself. The more he thought about taking the entrepreneurial leap, the more enthused he became. The potential success of this innovation, he felt, was tremendous. However, Wisdom needed both financial and advisory help. Larry Savage could provide both, so he and Wisdom agreed to set up a firm for the express purpose of negotiating a deal with Ed Phillips to market the Gourmet Cooker. Finding Phillips agreeable to their proposal, they immediately hired a patent lawyer to research the product and a corporation attorney to draw up a licensing agreement and to get them incorporated with an initial capitalization of $10,000. They traveled to Southern Illinois to negotiate a deal between Phillips and their new corporation. Allwood Chef, Inc., was on its way.

Questions

1. Identify every conceivable unique feature of the new product and translate these into consumer benefits. (See Exhibit 12-1.)
2. Determine the best market position for the new cooker.
3. Develop an alternative name for the new product.
4. Develop a two-step space ad for placement in a magazine that asks consumers to clip and send a coupon for more information.
5. Develop a brochure to send to people who return the coupons asking for more information.
6. Develop a sales letter to send with the brochure to people who have asked for information.
7. Develop a breakeven analysis based on assumed costs of marketing and distributing such a product by direct mail.

Materials in this case used by permission of SEI.

Direct Marketing Cases for Business-to-Business and Industrial Products and Services

The use of direct marketing to make complete sales is much more prominent in the consumer products sector than in the industrial or business-to-business products sector, where the use of direct marketing to perform specialized functions in the sales cycle, such as lead generation, qualification, etc., are primary and growing applications of the technique.

This trend in business-to-business marketing continues unabated as the cost of selling by traditional methods continues to escalate, motivating sellers to seek greater efficiency in their marketing programs—efficiency that is provided by direct marketing tools and techniques.

These sought-after efficiencies come largely from improvements in the generation and qualification of business-to-business leads. Accordingly, this section focuses on and illustrates the problems and challenges of generating leads with trade magazine advertising or other approaches, such as mail and/or telephone, as well as qualifying leads cost-effectively and/or moving them further along in the sales cycle.

Generating leads with creative mailings is vividly portrayed in the *Sealant Specialties Corporation* case and also *Advertising Specialties by Mail,* a particularly effective case for understanding the challenges presented when developing a creative platform for a targeted market. These cases are complemented by *Reliable Bearings, Keowee Grinding Machine Co.,* and *Blue Chip Grinding Machine Co.,* all of which focus on using telemarketing creatively to make direct marketing promotions more efficient and less expensive.

Finally, *Bar Codes, Unlimited: Selling Film Masters by Mail* offers a detailed illustration of all the elements of business-to-business direct marketing. The extensive detail provided in the case permits users to actually develop a total direct marketing package, calling on all of their skills of list selection, lead generation, and letter copy writing learned from earlier cases while also challenging them to consider the neglected but important direct response area of fulfillment.

Case 13   Sealant Specialties Corporation
Test Marketing an Industrial Product

Sealant Specialties Corporation developed a window crack (joint) filler that was easy to use, long-lasting, and attractive in appearance. It successfully marketed this product in bulk to manufacturers of windows, all of whom produced windows by the thousands and all of whom already owned the proper product application equipment.

The product manager for the product thought there must be a profitable market for the product among small storm door and storm window fabricators and applicators—firms that sold a few hundred windows a year perhaps, but normally no more at any one time than enough to equip one or two houses. Because of their size, he was sure that this market would buy only if a self-contained application gun were supplied as part of the product, and this feature was added.

The problem, it seemed, was how to test the market, how to reach and sell relatively small home improvement contractors economically, and how to keep the start-up investment low.

The number of such applicators in the three-state area surrounding the firm's main location was estimated to be a few hundred at best. The manager also determined that there were 120 prospects within 60 miles of the main plant.

The product manager first tried selling the product by making cold personal sales calls on prospects, but results were poor. Too often, the buyer was "out on a job," "already using a satisfactory sealant," or not interested "at this time of the year."

In view of this, it was decided to try a direct mail campaign.

The mailing went out in two stages. The first consisted of an inexpensive white folder, sealed with an adhesive bandage. The message said the offer would be in the next mailing.

The second mailing consisted of an inexpensive blue folder, also sealed with an adhesive bandage. The recipient was invited to use an 800 number to take advantage of a demonstration and to receive a free first-aid kit.

Success was to be measured by the number of sales appointments made. It was hoped that prospects would see the first-aid kit as a valuable incentive, for which they would be readily willing to trade a few minutes of time listening to a salesperson.

Questions

1. Discuss the motivation for an industrial firm to enter the direct-response channel.
2. Evaluate the probable effectiveness of this test program.
3. What other strategies and offers might have been considered?

This case was prepared by Roger W. Brucker, Odiorne Industrial Advertising.

Case 14

Reliable Bearings
Industrial Direct Marketing

Reliable Bearings Corporation manufactures tapered roller bearings for many kinds of machines such as off-road machinery, construction equipment, and chemical process equipment. The sales manager, Jim Race, had grown increasingly apprehensive about the increase in usage of foreign bearings. He decided to put together a combination sales and technical presentation, a "road show" that could be staged for larger customers and prospects in their plants.

The seminar presentation would highlight new developments in Reliable's product line, its investment in a new steel mill, the findings of a technical study of bearing life improvement, tips on how to apply different kinds of bearings in various designs, and finally a practical analysis of defects found in some of the foreign bearings.

The problem was how to get invitations to put on the seminar. Race asked a key salesman if he would spread the word about the availability of the seminar to his customers and prospects as he called on them. "I know my customers," said Sam Smooth, salesman for the Michigan territory. "If they hear I want to bring something like that in, they'll claim it's just a sales pitch for Reliable Bearings. I'm not going to destroy my credibility with them that way."

"Direct mail might work," said the advertising manager. "If we have an attractive brochure describing the seminar and enclose a return postcard for the names of those who want to attend, we should get an audience."

"Why not try telemarketing?" said the marketing manager. You get some silver-tongued persuader on the phone, and I'll bet you can talk lots of prospects into attending the seminar."

Race considered the three alternatives: He could force the sales staff to issue invitations, but at what cost? He might prepare a direct mailing, but would it work? Could a telemarketer explain enough on the telephone to get anyone to accept a seminar invitation?

While he was considering these alternatives the advertising manager stopped by to say he had purchased a Dun and Bradstreet mailing list of companies employing 100 or more within the top 10 SIC groups that use roller bearings in their products. "It's a good list. It has the name and telephone number of the chief engineer, exact title, company, address, city, state, and zip code," said the advertising manager. "I figure that whether you use direct mail or telemarketing that list will be useful to you."

Questions

1. What should Jim Race do next?
2. What steps might reduce the risk and increase the reward to Reliable Bearings in its effort to hold seminars in customer and prospect plants?
3. Prepare some materials that would be useful in getting the program rolling.
4. Develop a generic script for use by Reliable Bearings to sell its seminars.

This case was prepared by Roger W. Brucker, Odiorne Industrial Advertising.

Case 15   Keowee Grinding Machine Co.
Qualifying Requests for Quotations

Keowee Grinding Machine Company was a manufacturer of machines designed to grind cylinders—any kind of cylinder including step, thread, and tapered cylinders. Customers bought Keowee's machines to grind pump shafts, compressor shafts, hydraulic valve spools, engine crank shafts, and the like. These machines ranged in price from $150,000 to $300,000.

In early 1987, Keowee began to experience a difficult and expensive marketing problem. Although Keowee's machines were standardized to a degree, no two customers had exactly the same application, resulting in significant customization in virtually every case. Still, the company had to offer price information up front. This was not as simple a problem as it seemed to be.

Early on in the informing stage of marketing, prospects usually asked for an approximate price, which presented no major problem. But very frequently, prospects would ask for a quotation. A quotation is a formalized step in the negotiation process, usually undertaken after the prospect has become informed about the product's features, advantages, and benefits (usually by a sales rep or mailing pieces). It was the preparation of these formal quotations that was turning into a major marketing cost problem.

According to President Jeff Ridge, "When prospects ask us for a quotation on the price of a grinding machine we build, that's a two-day ordeal, requiring careful analysis of the job, proper technical recommendation, and selection of the proper accessories. And if we leave anything out, it could cost us thousands of dollars."

On the other hand, Ridge could not recall any customer ever buying exactly what was specified in the original, costly quotation. "As we get into the application we find that an accessory here and an option there will do a better job. The customer, when convinced, agrees. Oftentimes, too, items have to be cut out to save money, or added to meet a specific performance requirement."

According to Ridge, "Our problem is, how can we shortcut our time and money investment in making formal quotations that are never an accurate description of the final order?"

To solve this problem, the company decided to conduct a survey that probed how customers and prospects made use of quotations in their buying process. This survey revealed some useful information, as follows:

- A few prospects recognized that if they asked for a quotation the salesman would go away for a while. For them, their request was a brush-off.
- Most customers and prospects recognized that quotation preparation would be a substantial undertaking. They needed the quotation figure primarily for internal planning, budgeting, and justification—not for making the ultimate buy decision. They fully expected to be involved in an ongoing negotiation of details, and to pay either more or less than the quoted figure.
- A few customers had already received a quotation from one or more competitors. For them, the quotation was a key element in the justification process for a decision that had already been made to buy the competitive product.

Knowing these facts, marketing management decided to qualify prospects with a telemarketing program.

This required a script designed to learn what the prospect had in mind when asking for a quotation. Was the request a brush-off? Was only "ballpark" information needed? Was this request part of a head-to-head competitive decision situation in which only a detailed quotation would serve?

Management also reviewed the company's 50 most recent orders. They divided the final prices on these orders by the machines' shipping weights. This data, when plotted, revealed that very light and very heavy machines were very expensive per pound, and the per-pound price of intermediate-weight machines was typically much lower.

The information from the price-per-pound analysis was then used as the basis for a script strategy designed to separate legitimate grinding machine prospects from "tire kickers" who were less likely to purchase. The script language included "Can we discuss price for a minute? We made a study of our last 50 machines shipped. Our machines tend to be 30 percent to 40 percent heavier than competitive machines, which is one secret of our rigidity and accuracy. These machines price out at $12.50 per pound on the average. In your case, we guess your machine will weigh about 8,000 pounds. If that's true, we'd be looking at a price around $100,000. Is that reasonable for doing a good job in your application?"

The company also created boiler-plate "letterhead" or short-form quotations for use with prospects identified by telemarketing as being more likely prospects. But expensive, detailed, formal quotations were reserved for those situations identified through telemarketing as requiring them.

Questions

1. What is the problem in this case?
2. Evaluate the Keowee program. Will it work? Why or why not?
2. How can the program be improved?
3. Develop a generic script for use in responding to written or telephone requests for quotations.

This case was prepared by Roger W. Brucker, Odiorne Industrial Advertising.

Case 16

Blue Chip Grinding Machine Co.

Standardizing a Demonstration—Increasing Direct Marketing's Role

Blue Chip Grinding Machine Company complained that prospect requests for machine demonstrations were becoming a serious problem. Ten demos were already backlogged. Each demo required careful planning, review of the prospect's part prints, development of fixturing, working out the grinding process, dressing the grinding wheel, and writing a CNC program. Only experts could do all this.

"This problem is acute because no prospect will buy our machine without witnessing a demo. They want to know if our machine will do the work, "said George Moore, president of Blue Chip. He explained further that the best experts at staging demos were already working overtime on production. "We can't use just anybody, because if there is a hitch in the demo, the prospect may lose confidence and not buy."

The problem was how to solve this demonstration problem without hiring some people.

Moore decided to call in some consultants, who came up with the following report. Read the report and determine whether or not it should be implemented, and why.

Consultants' Proposal for Solving the Demo Problem

Objectives:

1. Reduce the costly aspects of demos—custom process development, custom tooling, special wheel procurement, personnel time, entertaining, and so on.
2. Use machine demonstration as a positive marketing tool to qualify prospects and shorten sales-order lead time.

Present Situation:

1. Machine demos with customer parts require lengthy analysis, preparation, setup, and run time.
2. Time spent on individual demos is time unavailable for other tasks.

3. Lengthy delays and backlog may raise questions about Blue Chip's capability, and thus may alienate prospects.

4. Any hitch in the demo proceedings, such as bad programs or parts, can postpone or kill the sale.

5. If higher-ranking buying influences do not attend the demo, they may offer additional questions and issues, further delaying the sale.

6. Machine tool buyers and salespeople want to see a demonstration to be assured of reliability and capability to fully satisfy the critical aspects of their application. (See the Appendix at the end of this case for consultants' interviews with buyers and salespeople.)

7. Sales leads from old customers, advertising, publicity, and trade shows are being qualified quickly with a telemarketing script. Reps have sufficient information for on-target follow-up. For qualified prospects they can supply data sheets to show how Blue Chip has solved similar problems. The stage is set for obtaining the prospect's part prints, presenting the demo part, and inviting the prospect for a demo visit.

Proposal:

1. *Adopt a preemptive demonstration strategy.* Try to persuade the prospect to attend a demonstration before the quotation is prepared, or as early as possible in the sales negotiation. This is to qualify the prospect and get him involved in a substantial way before he requests a demo running his own parts.

2. *Use a telemarketing script to force the demonstration and to find the key elements of reliability, the critical aspects of the application, and the buying influence.* The script provided in Exhibit 16-1 can be used by sales reps. The objective is to schedule a standard demonstration at the earliest possible time to head off the need for a special demonstration with customer parts.

3. *Organize a standard demonstration around two or three parts.* These should be selected to show machine capability in relation to the prospect's needs. The prospect is never told these parts are standard. Rather, the prospect's part print is examined, then the prospect is given the part to touch and examine and is told, "We want to demonstrate the critical elements for you in person. You will see first-hand our ability to hold this kind of tolerance (concentricity, steps, and so on). The plant demo also includes presentation modules by Blue Chip engineers in response to specifically identified reliability concerns (rigidity, repeatability, hydraulics, and so on).

Exhibit 16-1   Script to Schedule Demonstration

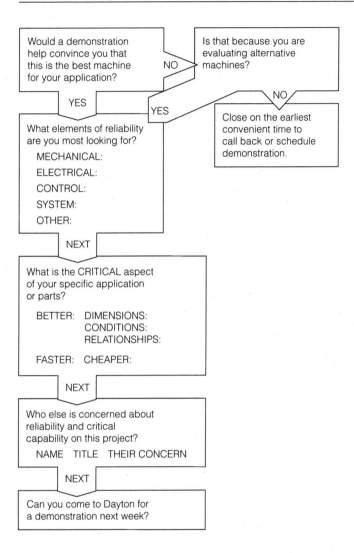

4. *Hand the prospect a videocassette of the demo for review back at the home plant.* Set up a video cart consisting of two VCRs, a camera, and a small color monitor. Tape the prospect's demo. The beginning of the tape includes some standard material on Blue Chip's capability. The prospect will show this tangible evidence of the demo to buyers at home that our salespeople may not be able to reach. Equipment cost is around $2000 total.

Benefits of the Proposal:

The benefits of this demonstration procedure include the following:

1. It qualifies prospects quickly. Willingness of a company to spend time and money to send its people is a good indicator of genuine intent to buy. Reps can call back to arrange a later demo when need is farther down the road.
2. It simplifies the demo procedure by standardization.
3. An early demo permits a faster demo, uncomplicated by having to work on nonstandard parts.
4. It provides hard evidence for the prospects' superiors and coworkers.
5. It sets up the "actual parts" demo as something extraordinary. The policy is to charge for an extraordinary demo and to give a credit against machine purchase.
6. It places the competition at a disadvantage. (Can the competitor make Blue Chip's demo part?) The prospects place their orders with people they have met, confident of capability and reliability.
7. It can head off competition by quickly engaging prospects with our solution. It can help sell special modifications to further differentiate our machine.
8. It shortens order lead time by shrinking the informing and negotiation stages of buying.
9. It should sell more machines yet require less lengthy interruptions of key personnel at Blue Chip because the demos are modular.

Recommended Action:

Decide on standard demo parts and prepare standard demos.

Current Sales Sequence:

Obtain leads from old customers, customers, advertising, publicity, and shows.

Qualify prospect using consultants' phone script.

Supply data sheets to prospect.

Receive prospect's part print for demo and request for quotation (RFQ).

Evaluate application, propose capability and reliability solution, and quote price.

Determine prospect's actual interest.

Conduct custom part demo at Dayton.

Negotiate the order if an order is obtained.

Proposed Sales Sequence:

Obtain sales leads from old customers, advertising, publicity, and shows.

Qualify prospect using consultants' phone script.

Supply data sheets to prospect.

Requalify prospect, schedule a standard demo by phone or rep, and receive part print.

Conduct a standard demo to establish capability and reliability; supply videocassette of demo to prospect.

Prepare a quote if one is requested.

Negotiate the order if an order is obtained.

Questions

1. What is the problem in this case?
2. Is this a direct marketing problem?
3. Should the consultants' proposal be implemented? Why or why not?

Appendix: Consultants' Interviews with Buyers and Salespeople

Interview with Gene Godfrey, Cortland Corp.

Roger Brucker is asking the questions and Gene Godfrey is answering.

Q: I'm trying to find out about how people like you use machine tool demonstrations when you are considering buying machine tools. Do you always ask for a demonstration?

A: Most of our machines are special. You often can't get a demonstration of something special. Now, if it's a standard machine, I want to see it. I want to talk to the user.

Q: What do you do with the results of the demonstration?

A: What do you mean?

Q: Do you make a formal written report, an oral report, or what?

A: It's a brief report to management. Sometimes I give them my notes. They may have some questions, and I may have to get more information. They're no dummies. Generally it's not a formal report. If it were government, I suppose there would be a long written report.

Q: If your report is favorable, they authorize the buy?

A: No, all purchasing is from headquarters. They sometimes overstep our recommendation. This is more likely on standard machines than on specials. They may have made a special buy or something we don't know about. Now, the hub of special machine builders is Detroit. Even so, we know that no special press is as good as a Minster. Minster supplies components to some of the special press people.

Q: What if your reaction to a demonstration is negative. What happens then?

A: Take Martin Machine down the street. We went over there to see a machine. The frame didn't seem heavy enough. It wasn't my project, so I don't know the whole story. But they went to Cincinnati for the grinder. I think it was a case of "too local"—that is, you have to go out of town to get the good stuff.

Q: Was there a written report on that conclusion?

A: No, it was reported verbally to management.

Q: How many layers of management do you report to on these demonstrations?

A: We report to the plant manager, without too many layers between. I report to my supervisor, who is primarily in quality, so he doesn't have a lot to say. His supervisor is third in command of this plant. He's plenty smart, so I'm always reporting to him, and he reports to the plant manager. The plant manager may challenge something, or he may just sign off on the buy. Often he'll say, "OK, if that's what you want, but you guys have to make it work."

Q: Why do production executives like you want a demonstration?

A: We want to see if the machine is reliable. How well built is it? What components do they use, and are they good? Like cylinders, valves, controls and so on. If those are not what we have standardized around here, we'll specify to use Vickers valves. You see, we have to standardize because otherwise we'd have to stock everybody's controls. We use Allen-Bradley on most machines, so we can stock those. I also check to see how things fit, whether the ways are generous, and whether it looks like it would hold up. In specials, I realize I won't see the machine we are discussing, but I want to be sure they can do the main thing.

Q: You mean the critical thing?

A: Yes, the thing that makes it special. I suppose there are some guys who like to go to demos to get a steak dinner. That may be the real motive in some cases.

Q: It's not your motivation?

A: (Laughs) No, I don't much like going out of town. We did have a rebuild that was my project. The rebuilder farmed the job out to a sister division plant in Portland, Maine. I went up there and had a good time. They stood by the lake and pointed to the island where President Bush had his home. If I had been there longer I might have seen it.

Q: Thank you, Gene, for your time. I appreciate it.

A: No trouble at all, Roger. Goodbye.

Interview with Bill Cardigan, Chief Manufacturing Engineer, Chemical Equipment, Inc.

Bill Brown is asking the questions, Bill Cardigan is answering.

Q: Do you ever ask for a demonstration on a particular part when you are buying a machine tool?

A: We have a design for a very simple part, a cylindrical piece with a couple of steps, that we ask them to set up for. We supply the tooling, and the process information, and the material to run 25 parts. We ask the vendor to program the machine that he proposes for this work and to run 25 of them, in our presence, without interference from engineers. We number the parts as they come off, and time the cycle. We examine the parts for drifting from specification, and for finish.

I realize this takes a lot of time and money on the vendors' part, but our experience has shown that this assures us the cycle time and quality we need.

Some machine buyers can be satisfied with a standard demonstration, where the machine tool builder shows special parts of his own choosing being made. These parts always show the machine off to its best advantage, and if the buyer is sharp, he can determine whether this machine is good at the part he wants to make on the machine in question. Chemical Products, Inc. prefers the more elaborate and time-consuming way. Chemical Products, Inc. will ask three or four vendors to do this same demonstration.

Q: What do you look for in a demonstration?

A: Reliability, consistency, repeatability, and predictability. Reliability is the most important thing. We assume that all machines are rugged, that all control systems can do the same things, and that electrical and hydraulic systems are essentially the same among vendors. We generally buy turning centers, NC lathes and drills—all fairly standard machines available from a number of sources. There is never any question as to whether the machine can do the job. The questions are "How reliably?" and "How fast?"

Q: After a demonstration, to whom do you report?

A: I don't have to make a report internally. The vendor usually asks me to write up the results of the demonstration, which I do and file a copy of this report in the folder on the purchase of this machine and give a copy to the vendor, not identifying his competition.

Q: Is there anything else you'd like to tell me?

A: A machine vendor should develop a standard demonstration and try to use it when it will satisfy the needs of the prospect. Many buyers can look at a part slightly different than their own and assure themselves that the machine will do what the quotation says it will do.

For a builder to offer to build the machine and guarantee that it will produce as promised is bad business for both builder and buyer.

I always call other purchasers of this type machine and ask them what their experience has been.

Vendors always resist doing demonstrations, and sometimes ask to be reimbursed for the trouble. I usually tell them that the competitors have offered to do it free, and that solves the problem. I don't know what I'd do if they all wanted to charge.

Interview with Waldemar Gould, Former Sales Manager for New Age Machine Company, a Blue Chip Competitor

Bill Brown is asking the questions, Waldemar Gould is answering.

Q: Did you do demonstrations for prospects?

A: Yes. We generally had to use a machine that was being built for someone else, as we did not have a stock of "demonstrators" available. Sometimes we did not have the exact model he was going to buy, but he would accept a part being run on a different model. Sometimes we could run parts for which we were building the tooling, but sometimes we had to run his specific part. For the automotive industry we always had to run off 75 or more parts when the machine was finished, so the customer could verify the dimensional accuracy of the machine before it left our plant.

We sometimes charged for the presale demonstration and credited this against the cost of the machine if the prospect bought. Otherwise we billed him. The tooling could be pretty expensive and not usable for anything else.

Q: What did prospects look for in a demonstration?

A: They looked at the quality of the part.

Q: To whom did the witnesses at the demonstration report?

A: The witnesses were generally manufacturing engineers and they made a written report to the chief manufacturing engineer in large plants and the plant manager in smaller plants. The latter was the person who made the buying decision.

Q: Is there anything else you'd like to tell me?

A: Screw machines are different from crush grinders. Most people know the quality they'll get from a screw machine, but they aren't sure about a grinder. Consequently it may be more difficult for Blue Chip to sell without a demonstration on the actual part than for New Age. Another way to provide a demonstration is to take the prospect to a satisfied customer, and let him see the machine in action on someone else's part. Sometimes this is hard to arrange.

This case was prepared by Roger W. Brucker, Odiorne Industrial Advertising.

Case 17   Bar Codes, Unlimited
Selling Film Masters by Mail

Everyone is familiar with bar codes—those inch-long groupings of thick and thin black lines. Bar codes are used to quickly and accurately communicate product or item identification through electronic media. Bar codes help video store owners solve a major headache—keeping track of hundreds of movie cassettes. They help bookstores and book departments decrease cash inventory even while sales rise, by helping track thousands of titles quickly and easily. Professional offices such as those of lawyers, doctors, and accountants use bar codes to bill time and to track client/patient documents that get passed around. Dosage control via bar coding is spreading rapidly in hospitals. The post office is installing a massive bar code sorting system aimed at cutting costs and improving the speed and accuracy of mail delivery. A major wood products manufacturer is planning to affix color-coded, pressure-sensitive Universal Product Code (UPC) labels on the ends of pieces of lumber. The airline industry uses bar codes to sort and track luggage more efficiently and accurately. And, penetration of bar coding in the food retailing industry, where it began, is nearly complete.

Bar Codes, Unlimited

One supplier to the bar coding industry is Bar Codes, Unlimited, a small Dayton, Ohio operation started by Jay Dring in 1989. Prior to launching Bar Codes, Unlimited, Jay Dring had over 27 years of retail experience, including ownership of his own retail store and 18 years in sales with NCR corporation. In 1974, while with NCR, Jay helped introduce the Uniform Product Code symbol scanning system to the retail industry. In fact, he was a major player in the world's very first bar code scanner installation in Marsh Supermarkets in Troy, Ohio, in 1974. Since then, he has been involved with thousands of other installations. All of Bar Codes, Unlimited's current business is developed through personal selling. Jay Dring now wants to test the viability of the direct-response channel as the next step in his company's approach to marketing its products and services.

The Universal Product Code

The key to the universal product code is its machine-readable bar code symbol for the 12-digit, all numeric code. This number is represented by a series of parallel light spaces and dark bars which can be read by an optical scanner at the checkout stand. The code number permits a computer to recognize the item. In most applications, there is no price or other information in the number. Instead, when read, the code number is sent to an in-store or remote computer that contains constantly updated information, including price, on all items that are carried in the store, or are being monitored for other reasons. The computer transmits back to the checkout stand or other input point the item's price and description (which are instantly displayed on the customer's receipt tape) as well as relevant information on taxability, food stamp acceptance, and so on. While doing this, the computer also captures and stores item movement information that can be aggregated, instantly compared or checked against other data, or analyzed and summarized in a wide variety of control reports.

Film Masters

Film masters are the central ingredient in the bar coding process and are usually required whether the bar code will be printed directly onto a package label or onto pressure-sensitive labels that are later affixed to the package. Film masters are most easily understood as the bar code numbers translated into artwork. Technically, a film master is a negative or positive image of a Universal Product Code symbol that allows reproduction of the symbol. Because these are used to make printing plates, film masters are a critical element in any successful application of bar coding. The quality of the film master determines whether, and to what extent, the printed symbol will be scannable. Thus, if the translation from number to film master or artwork form is not done according to very strict rules, much can, and usually will, go wrong.

Bar codes are usually printed either on adhesive labels or directly onto the product's packaging. Accordingly, poor bar coding quality results mainly from flaws either in adhesive labels or in the film masters used when printing adhesive labels or product packaging. A goof in either can be a major problem. For example, adhesive labels that customers can readily peel off will, in fact, be peeled off by some customers. Some of these may even be placed on other merchandise as a way of getting the other merchandise for a lower price. Significant problems can also result when adhesive labels do not adhere. For example, labels fell off a significant percentage of 50,000 packages of frozen smoked fish, making the tracking of this perishable product very difficult. Incorrect or unreadable codes can be a nightmare of cost and wasted time. To see how a flawed film master adds up to a disaster for the brand's owner, one need only imagine a million units of a nationally branded item rendered untrackable by an unreadable UPC code symbol printed from a plate produced from a flawed film master.

Uniform Code Council

The chronology of events leading up to the present-day widespread use of bar code technology and the Universal Product Code (UPC) dates back to the earliest days of retail chains. Rapid expansion of use began when the National Association of Food Chains initiated development of the UPC in 1969. Part of this included the establishment of an organization to act as a clearinghouse for manufacturers, retailers, and wholesalers participating in the system. This organization, the Uniform Code Council, Inc., headquartered in Dayton, Ohio is not a government agency. It is a private, voluntary organization formed specifically to control the issuing of manufacturers' code numbers, to provide detailed UPC information, and to provide worldwide coordination of bar coding for all member participants. The council's growing list of major sponsoring organizations include the Food Marketing Institute, the Grocery Manufacturers of America, the National American Wholesale Grocers' Association, the National Food Brokers' Association, and the National Grocers' Association.

Whenever a producer decides to sell a product through retail channels that use bar code scanners at their checkouts, a unique six-digit universal product code number that identifies the manufacturer must be obtained from the Uniform Code Council. (There is a one-time fee for this number that is based on retail sales volume and is a minimum of $300.) A five-digit number that identifies the specific item and a twelfth check-digit are added by the manufacturer or other number recipient. For example, the Crest toothpaste bar code number is 0 37000 00334 2. The UPC-authorized unique number for the manufacturer, Procter and Gamble, is 0 37000. The item number, unique within Procter and Gamble's product line and added by Procter and Gamble, is 00334. The 2 is a check-digit. Scanners read the symbol, and not the number printed below it. Thus, it is always the readability of the symbol rather than the number that is at issue.

The above description is of the "A" version of the UPC symbol. What is actually seen on the Crest toothpaste package is another version called the "E" symbol, with the number shown as 0 373340 2 rather than 0 37000 00334 2. Some of the zeros in the number have been suppressed. The "E" symbol is used on smaller products where there is limited space for the symbol. The "E" version is constructed following the same rules as the "A" version and differs from it only in that some or all of the zeros in the "A" version code number are suppressed. This permits the symbol to be physically shorter without loss of information.

In either the "A" or the "E" case, the symbol must be printed to strict specifications, both as to size and location. The "nominal" size is 1.020 inches high and 1.469 inches wide. This can be varied from 80 percent of nominal to 200 percent of nominal. No reduction, or expansion, beyond that shown in the *UPC Symbol Specification Manual* (a publication of the Uniform Code Council) is permitted. Violation of this rule can lead to poor scanning quality.

Placement of the code on the product package is also critical because the more variation there is in symbol location, the more difficulty the checkout clerk will have in finding the symbol to pass it across the scanner. The Uniform Code Council supplies a manual entitled *UPC Symbol Location Guidelines,* that provides detailed, uniform rules for doing this.

The Uniform Code Council is not directly involved in the creation of film masters. It provides only manuals. Translating the code number into a machine-readable bar code symbol to appear on its products' packages is totally the responsibility of the manufacturer. However, the council stands ready to provide additional informational assistance to ensure that the number holder gets the bar code properly produced. This assistance includes offering new members lists of film master suppliers, lists of manufacturers of UPC label printing equipment, and lists of bar code consultants.

Printers and Film Masters

Film masters have to be made in different specifications depending on whether flexography, gravure, or silkscreen printing will be used. For example, when using silkscreen, the printing process reproduces exactly what the film master dictates. However, if the printing is to be done using flexography, which uses a rubber plate, the pressure of the press will enlarge the bar code bars. To compensate for this, the plate bars must be smaller than the bar code specifications indicate. To make this happen, the film master must be correspondingly reduced so that plates made from them print correctly sized bar codes. These and other complexities motivate a majority of printers not to get involved in film master creation. As a result, users are often left with the responsibility for supplying their packaging or adhesive label printers with the film master. Users, in turn, nearly always find it cost-effective and expedient to turn to external suppliers for such services. More than 100 companies are offering film master services. Among these was Jay Dring's firm, Bar Codes, Unlimited.

Bar Codes, Unlimited's Current Products

Neither film masters nor adhesive labels are actually produced by Bar Codes, Unlimited. Rather, Bar Codes, Unlimited serves as a bar code consultant and nationwide middleman or distributor for firms that produce the film masters and adhesive labels. The company also serves both customers and suppliers as a kind of consultant-broker and quality control agency, making sure that the supplier produces film masters and/or adhesive labels to exacting specifications for every customer. This, of course, demands a close working relationship with the suppliers. Dring has clearly established such a relationship, and his fledgling company appears to be well on its way to success. Projected company sales, all of which are being made via direct personal contact by Dring, are approximately $150,000 for the current fiscal year. At this time the firm has only two employees: Dring and a secretary.

Bar Codes, Unlimited's Current Markets

The Food and Pharmaceutical Market

Jay Dring's background and thorough familiarity with the checkout and scanning industry gave him instant credibility with several national chains in the food and pharmaceutical industries. He chose to concentrate on these initially, selling them in person. Although film masters are a part of nearly every sale, adhesive labels are the most profitable part of his business.

Third Party Sales

Dring also has had some success selling automotive accessory, food, and drug trade associations on third-party marketing of film masters and adhesive labels to their memberships. Third-party marketing is a big business that involves selling the membership of a trade or other association under the auspices of the association. The buyer does business with the trade association, but the product or service is supplied by a third party. There are thousands of trade associations across the country. It appears, therefore, that these associations represent a very large and attractive market.

New Markets with Direct Marketing Potential

As he continues to develop the food chains, trade associations, and pharmaceutical markets with in-person selling, Dring, like most good entrepreneurs, has begun to cast about for other markets and marketing approaches. Inspired by a continuing flow of new applicants for UPC numbers, Dring has turned to direct mail as a method to get better leads from his current markets and possibly to make direct sales to others.

The Uniform Code Council New Applicant List

Each month approximately 800 applications for new UPC numbers are received by the Uniform Code Council in Dayton. When the applicant plans to print the symbol on a product's package, and often when it has to be printed on adhesive labels (labels can be done without film masters by many printing devices), a film master must be made for each of the products that the applicant plans to sell through a channel using bar code scanning. The names of the companies that submitted applications during preceding months can be purchased from the Uniform Code Council for $.10 per name and used as a direct mail list.

There is, necessarily, a time lag between the time the applicants get numbers and the time the Uniform Code Council can make their names available. The Uniform Code Council has a waiting period of two weeks before the names are made available. This delay works to allow a new UCC member to get the number and all UCC manuals before being solicited by film master suppliers. Thus, if a film master supplier buys the names every month, he or she would receive names of members who joined the UCC between two and six weeks prior. By the time Bar Codes, Unlimited receives the names, many of the applicants have already transformed their UPC numbers into film masters and onto their packages. Nonetheless, for one reason or another, even after as long as six weeks, a sizable percentage of this list is still in the market for film masters, adhesive labels, or consulting.

The Uniform Code Council list is not well defined. It is Dring's general belief that the list contains a high percentage of "mom and pops" selling anything from cookies to ginseng root. Small, but more sophisticated entrepreneurs, and large companies selling new products through bar code scanning channels, are also thought to be prominent on the list. In sum, at the beginning of Dring's investigation, no one at Bar Codes, Unlimited knew for sure who would be on a typical new list of applicants.

The Uniform Code Council also markets lists by category such as pharmaceutical, industrial, and apparel, as well as several subsets of food and grocery manufacturers. Some of these lists number into the thousands. The purchase of a complete category list would enable Dring to approach all companies (or select companies within a category) known to have a Universal Product Code Number.

Printers

On occasion, commercial printers and platemakers are competitors to Bar Codes, Unlimited, but more often than not, both are also significant markets. New UPC recipients often turn first to their printers for help in translating their new UPC numbers into symbols. Printers, in turn, not generally being specialists in the film master business but requiring a film master before they can proceed, often turn to someone else, such as Bar Codes, Unlimited for the service. Dring realized that these printers could be a major market for his services and that they would require unique promotions.

Packaged-Goods Sellers

Dring was also interested in an effort on the part of some major packaged-goods sellers to use bar codes to assess and increase the effectiveness of their promotional efforts. For example, a dog-food seller promoted his dog food with specialized bar codes on the package. Contest entrants were asked to place these on an entry form. When these were turned in for prizes, the seller could learn much about the who, what, when, and where of his dog-food buyers. Initially, Dring was unclear as to exactly how this process worked, or even all of its purposes, but given the enormous amount of promotion going on in the packaged-goods industry, it sounded very promising to him.

Other Markets

It soon became apparent to Dring that bar coding was rapidly becoming used by many other industries, and that although these industries might not be his most promising initial markets, they were certainly worth watching and contacting as soon as his resources permitted. Among those he noted were the hardware, home accessory, lumber, and airline industries and the post office.

Competitor Activity

All of Dring's markets were being pursued by a variety of direct mail competitors. He knew that at least 13 of the firms pursuing the UPC applicants were doing current mailings because a friend of his had obtained a number for his product line and received 13 different mailings offering him film master and related services. It was clear from the timing of the receipt of these mailings that all were buying the Uniform Code Council list and mailing it just as Dring planned to do.

Examination of these mailers revealed a variety of approaches. Some asked for orders; other invited inquiries.

One of the simplest of these packages was a postcard. It had a bar code symbol on the top center of the front. Below this it had the firm's 800 number printed in large, bold print. On the back it had a sample bar code adhesive label, which led the eyes of the reader into a very simple message: the firm was a qualified supplier of UPC bar code film masters and had been informed that the addressee had been assigned a manufacturer's number. It went on to stipulate a vague "starting" per-unit price and invited the addressee to call the 800 number for a quote. The other mailings ranged along a continuum of complexity all the way to one that came in an 8½-by-11-inch envelope containing an expensive brochure, a sales letter, several sample film masters, an order form, and even a small pamphlet analyzing when the use of bar codes was the right thing for a business to do.

All of the mailers offered quick turnaround on receipt of an order. Their prices ranged, or appeared to range, from $10 to $35 per film master. Exactly what could be received for the stated price could not be known until the recipient accepted the mailer's invitation to call and discuss the firm's services and prices.

Changes in the Competitive Environment

In 1986 the typical firm offering film master services was run by a highly technical person who knew the bar code system and business thoroughly. At that time, bar code services were priced much higher, with film masters, for example, being sold for as much as $100 or more. Few mistakes were made by these suppliers because they knew what they were doing. Now, however, the field has attracted a large number of firms that some have termed "fly-by-nighters," who have only a very superficial knowledge of the technical details of the business, and in some cases no real idea of what they are doing. This has driven both the prices and quality of bar code services down and made the industry very competitive. This is particularly true when buyers can be convinced that one film master company is the same as any other, making price the only issue. This is untrue, but buyers often believe it.

Economics of the Industry

Most of the firms on the UCC new-applicant list are believed to be small; otherwise they would already have a bar code number and a well-established bar coding system. Many of them are also believed to have only a few items, and most probably have only one or two items to be bar coded. Thus, the typical prospect on the list would need only one or two film masters. This distills down to a very simple fact: there isn't much profit to be had selling film masters one at a time to this list, even at Bar Codes, Unlimited's current price of $19.95 for one film master.

Bar Codes, Unlimited's average film master production costs are in the $3 to $6 range, with the average production and warehousing cost per unit being about $5. The gross profit or marketing margin is, therefore, approximately $15 per unit. Economies of scale are present but very marginal in the production of film masters.

Low profit on film masters is offset by potential profits from adhesive labels and consulting. The situation most of the new bar code number applicants find themselves in—having existing inventories without bar codes on printed labels—requires initial use of adhesive labels rather than printing directly onto the product package. Adhesive label orders can be very profitable. For example, one book printer had 500,000 books with incorrect bar codes and had to purchase adhesive labels to place over the original incorrect ones. Adhesive label orders from the new applicant list are estimated to fall for the most part in the 5,000 to 50,000 label range.

Adhesive label costs to Bar Codes, Unlimited are in the following ranges:

Quantity	Cost per Thousand
1,000–5,000	$17.00–22.00, average $18.50
5,000–10,000	$11.00–17.00, average $14.00
10,000–25,000	$3.00–6.00, average $4.50
25,000–50,000	$1.50–3.00, average $2.25

Prices correspond to costs and normally reflect a 100 percent markup on costs. For example, an order for 12,000 labels might be priced at $9.00 per thousand.

Current Direct Marketing Program Status

Dring's initial direct mail effort consisted of the letter shown in Exhibit 17-1. The initial response to this letter, when mailed to the Uniform Code Council list, was virtually nil. However, after several weeks had elapsed, some calls did come in from recipients and one of these turned into a significant sale. Dring thinks the results of his mailings should be much better and is thinking of consulting a direct marketing professional. Though he is not sure what a professional could know that could really help, he feels that there must be some way to use direct marketing to profitably access the Uniform Code Council list market.

Dring also has a near-term plan to generate leads among pharmaceutical companies. This could be a very profitable enterprise because pharmaceutical companies, which are already well-established users of bar code scanning, sometimes buy hundreds of film masters each month. Unfortunately, it is not easy to determine who in pharmaceutical companies buys film masters. Thus, at this point, Dring is confused as to how to go about generating leads in this industry. He feels, however, that the basic method should be direct response of some sort.

The pharmaceutical company market, like most other markets, has many firms that already have UPC numbers. Thus, high-potential

Exhibit 17-1   Dring's Initial Sales Letter to the Uniform Code Council's New Applicants

Bar Codes, Unlimited, Inc.
7651 East Von Dette Circle
Dayton, Ohio 45459
513-434-CODE

Dear U.P.C. Participant:

Your product is on the way to commercial success with the addition of
the UPC (Universal Product Code). Our firm is available to assist you in the
implementation of your UPC program. Bar Codes, Unlimited concentrates
on producing high-quality codes for a reasonable price and providing
prompt service. Inferior codes can cause your product to be rejected by
your customer.

Professional Services

- Film Masters
- UPC Consulting
- Implementation Planning
- Pressure Sensitive Labels

- Symbol Verification
- Prompt Service
- Reasonable Price
- Customer Satisfaction

In 1974, I introduced the first UPC symbol scanning system to the retail
industry as well as to federal and state agencies. My 27 years of retail experience have afforded me the opportunity to demonstrate and install hundreds
of scanning systems.

Bar Codes, Unlimited invites you to become a customer and grant us the
opportunity to fulfill all your UPC implementation needs.

John J. Dring
President

prospects in the pharmaceutical market and in the other markets
may or may not appear on the Uniform Code Council monthly lists.
Those that do not may represent higher potential customers than
those who do. Dring feels that his program for developing these markets may, therefore, have to include a specialized approach.

Current Ordering Procedures

At the present time, Bar Codes, Unlimited has only one incoming
telephone line. Calls on this line are handled by an electronic system that facilitates the receipt of fax orders but permits normal handling of other calls. Thus, when a fax call is received, the system
automatically directs it to the fax machine. But when a customer calls,
the system allows either Bar Codes, Unlimited or the caller to switch
the call to the fax line, eliminating the need to place another call.
Thus, after-hours customers can 1) Fax an order to Bar Codes, Un-

limited, 2) leave a recorded message, or 3) leave a recorded message and then fax an order or other information. Fax orders received by 7:30 p.m. one day can be turned around by 10:30 a.m. the next day if the customer's need is urgent.

First-time film master buyers do not need to see an order form, nor do they need detailed instructions. However, they do have to supply detailed application information. This would have to be collected over the phone whenever a first-time mail-order buyer is being serviced. (Repeat customers are supplied with copies of an order form for use when faxing repeat orders to Bar Codes, Unlimited.) Some of the directions for completing Bar Codes, Unlimited's necessarily complex order form are shown in Exhibit 17-2.

Dring's Dilemma

As he surveys his situation and options, John Dring is unsure of what to do. He is sure direct-response marketing can work, but he has tried it once and it did not work. He has decided to turn to an expert for assistance. You are the expert. Show him why and how direct marketing will work for him, or prove to him why another direct-response effort will be futile.

The authors wish to gratefully acknowledge a contributing author, Nabil Hassan, Professor, Wright State University.

Exhibit 17-2   Data Requested on Bar Codes, Unlimited's Order Form

On the "Date Needed" line, please be specific. Do not leave blank or use the terms "ASAP" or "RUSH." Our manufacturing system makes use of the needed date as its priority for manufacturing sequence.

UPC Version:
A—standard 10 digit version (excluding 1st and 12th digits)
E—zero suppression, 6 digit version (excluding 1st and 12th digits)

EAN Version: Standard 13 digit version (13th digit is for country). EAN stands for European Article Number.

Number System Character:
0, 6, 7—General merchandise items. 6 and 7 are also used in industrial applications.
2—variable weight items
3—national drug code
4—for retailer use without format restrictions
5—coupons
1, 8, and 9—not in use at this time

Flag Number: Please supply us flag numbers for EAN film master.

Check Character Number: Please calculate and supply us with the check character number. It will be verified by the manufacturing computer. Should it be incorrectly calculated or an error made in the writing of the order, the symbol will be made according to the first eleven numbers on the order. However, the notation "Check character NBR: X (changed from Y)" will appear in the check character number portion of the film master carrier.

2 and 5 Digit Supplements: For use within the paperback and periodical industry. Leave this space blank if you do not want a supplemental master.

Magnification: The decimal equivalent of the percentage of reduction or magnification. Example: .85 is a 15% reduction, 1.00 is nominal size, 1.23 is a 23% magnification. The magnification will be specified by your printer.

Bar Width: Bars may be reduced or grown. You must fill in this column to achieve reduction or growth. Example: .002 would be a two-thousandth reduction, .000 would be no bar width reduction.

Note: Printing method for bar width reduction.

- Offset: Minimum ½ thousandth to minus 3 thousandths
- Flexography: For straight rubber minus 3 thousandths to minus 6 thousandths; for photopolymer minus 1 thousandth to minus 3 thousandths
- Gravure: no bar width reduction
- Silkscreen: plus 2 thousandths

Negative (Neg.) or Positive (Pos.): Your printer will specify which of these is required.

Right Reading Emulsion, Up or Down: Your printer will specify which of these is required.

For Flexo Barrier: Check this column only if you want a flexographic barrier around the symbol. The barrier will replace the corner marks on the master.

Case 18

Advertising Specialties by Mail
Developing a Test Direct Marketing Plan

Tom and Jackie Ullmo, owners of S.E. Bennett Company, a successful advertising specialties company in Cleveland, Ohio, have been considering moving into the direct mail marketing business for some time. The magnet business card, an ad specialty product already sold by the S.E. Bennett Company, looks viable as a direct mail product.

Magnets are currently in wide use as carriers of advertising messages. Magnet business cards are flat magnets printed with the information normally found on paper business cards. Magnets, particularly emergency card magnets, are currently selling well for the Ullmos, but they are only one of thousands of ad specialty items their firm sells.

Organizations routinely hand out promotional items of all sorts, including magnet business cards, to their customers and prospects. Magnet business cards are offered for sale by virtually every ad specialty company in the country. Normally, however, they are just one of many items offered, and are typically not given specific merchandising attention.

Merchandising a product line in a direct mail package often brings success. In view of this, the Ullmos have decided to try selling magnets in the direct mail channel. Having tested the direct mail channel once before with another product without success, however, they fell they need a consultant to guide them through their next effort. You are that consultant. The Ullmos recognize how difficult it is to be successful in the direct-response channel but are sure that there is a way to make the direct-response channel work for them. Your task is to find that way.

The Product

Magnet suppliers offer a wide variety of magnet product options having the business card function as their essence. Among these are calendars, card holders, memo holders, memo boards, picture frames, rulers, memo pads, postcards, golf balls, mirrors, keys, doggie bones, teeth, telephones, hearts, coin shapes, cars, trucks, churches, books, school buses, light bulbs, states, eyeglasses, tickets, pizzas, credit cards, postcards, door hangers, roladex postcards, soft drink cans, and stop signs.

Suppliers offer all of their magnets in a preprinted form or in a design that permits the user to write in his or her own information such as emergency numbers (fire department, doctor, police, poison control, and so on) and other important telephone numbers. The magnets come in five colors: blue, red, green, yellow, or black. Up to four colors can be utilized on any one item. Most of the time, stock items that need only customer-specified printing are available; however, when clients want something special, customization to almost any specification can be obtained.

Business card magnets can be manufactured in either a stiff or flexible form. Stiff magnets can be shrink-wrapped, and both forms can be supplied in other unique package formats if the customer desires it. S.E. Bennett will be a reseller, rather than a manufacturer, of the magnets. Orders will be taken and resubmitted to magnet suppliers who will print, package, and ship the individual orders. The mailing process will indicate shipment from S.E. Bennett, permitting S.E. Bennett to own the seller-customer relationship.

The Market

At Tom's request, one magnet supplier provided some data concerning sales of magnets by industry. According to this supplier, the following is a list of the top ten users of write-on emergency number magnets based on their order history:

1 Hospitals
2 Real estate agents
3 Insurance agents
4 Schools
5 Pharmacies
6 Consumer products organizations
7 Media (radio stations, newspapers)
8 Communities or cities
9 Philanthropic organizations
10 Special events (Safety Awareness Week, Fire Safety Week, Education Week)

This same supplier also supplied data concerning the top ten markets for business cards magnets. These, not in rank order, are as follows:

• Real estate agents
• Insurance agents
• Medical professionals
• Service industry organizations
• Manufacturing organizations
• Financial institutions
• Transportation organizations

- Automotive organizations
- Food industry organizations
- Media (radio stations, newspapers)
- Construction organizations

In the ad specialty business, buyers are known to be prone to treat orders for less than $100 as impulse purchases. A major negative price-demand effect has been observed in the industry when the price of an offer passes $100. At this time, the causes of this price point are unclear.

Supplier Pricing

Suppliers' average suggested resale prices for magnets are indicated in Table 18-1. These prices are for items such as business cards averaging 2 by 3½ inches in size. Prices increase about 10 percent for each ½ square inch increase in size. Typical reseller markups are in the 40-to-50-percent range, with the average being about 45 percent.

Given the pricing data shown in Table 18-1 and an order of 300 business card magnets, Bennett's resale price would be approximately $100.00 ($0.33 × 300), and its gross profit would be $45.00 ($100.00 × .45). The minimum order size that suppliers are willing to fill is usually 250 magnets. As Table 18-1 shows, significant price breaks can be obtained from suppliers for larger quantities. Also, suppliers offer additional discounts of up to 10 percent for cooperative promotion expenses. These discounts should be readily available to S.E. Bennett, given their planned direct-response activity. In the example given, such discounts could add as much as $10.00 to the gross margin obtained on a $100.00 direct response order.

Tom Ullmo has been negotiating some purchase programs with various magnet suppliers. One of these programs involves the supplier accepting orders in groups of ten different 250-unit orders, each with at least one color imprint that is similar for the ten orders. The only change of copy would occur, for example, when ten orders come in for salespeople or dealers from a single company, with the only copy difference from one order to the next being the salesperson's or dealer's name and phone number. Under these conditions, S.E. Bennett would pay .102 cents per magnet and $8.40 per copy change. A second program sets the minimum order quantity at 500 and the price paid on 500 magnets at .114 cents per magnet with no charge for one color imprint and an $8.40 charge for each change of copy in the case of multiple orders from a single customer. If an S.E. Bennett direct marketing program is launched, it is nearly certain that suppliers will go along with these programs to help support the effort.

Table 18-1 Retail Price for Various Quantities of Magnets

	250	500	1000	2500	5000	10,000
Business card magnets	.33	.30	.25	.22	.19	.17
Stock flat flexible magnets	.51	.48	.34	.24	.21	
Write-on magnets	.51	.48	.34	.24	.21	
Custom flat flexible magnets						
Square Corners		—	—	.12	.10	.09
Round Corners		—	—	.34	.12	.11
Postcards with magnets (4 × 6")				.45	.31	.26
Rolodex with postcard magnets		—	—	.44	.39	.31
Hard plastic magnets	.75	.72	.68	.64	.51	
Magnetic mirrors	1.75	1.64	1.51	1.42		
Magnetic picture frames	.68	.64	.47	.37	.32	
Magnetic clip business cards	1.35	1.25	1.10	.95	.85	.52
Magnetic vinyl card holder	1.15	1.04	.80	.66	.59	
Magnetic rulers	.72	.68	.50	.41	.38	.35
Magnetic calendars	1.10	.98	.60	.42	.31	.26
Magnetic memo boards	1.44	1.33	1.19	1.10	1.03	

Ordering Processing

The Ullmos already have a functioning order-processing system in place at their Cleveland, Ohio offices. They will also install a toll-free 800 number, if needed, for order-taking purposes. Visa, Mastercard, and Discover procedures are in place to facilitate payment for orders. Thus, all that remains to be done, in addition to order generation, are 1) the creation of an order-processing system within the S.E. Bennett company, 2) the training of S.E. Bennett operators to know what to expect and what to say and do when these orders come in, and 3) the creation of a properly designed paperwork flow system.

Before most orders can be processed, a business card, letterhead, other graphic, or message copy must be obtained from the customer. Faxed representations are acceptable, but only when color information is not vital to accurate reproduction of the graphic on the magnet. When customers submit business cards with their orders, the business cards are considered "camera-ready" and no set-up fee is charged. On other submissions, such as letterheads, magnet suppliers charge S.E. Bennett a setup fee of from $20 to $25. Should orders come in asking for magnets for several different people within an organization that differ only by the name, phone number, and so on of each individual, suppliers will assess a $12 setup charge for each different individual.

Delivery, from the time an order is received at S.E. Bennett in Cleveland, ranges from three to four weeks. Orders can be shipped directly from the magnet supplier, rather than from S.E. Bennett. However, they should appear to be coming from S.E. Bennett.

Cost and Availability of Samples

Samples of promotional magnets such as emergency-number magnets can be obtained from suppliers for approximately 7 cents each. These are inexpensive because they become available whenever mistakes are made on orders and they have to be done over—for example, when wrong telephone numbers, misspelled names, or other flaws make orders unacceptable. Such samples might be usable for mailing to prospects, but they will not have been designed with any particular market in mind. S.E. Bennett can also buy specifically designed magnets for inclusion in direct mailings. These will cost at least 7 cents each and probably more.

Marketing Ad Specialty Magnets

Advertising specialty magnets are marketed by hundreds of advertising specialty companies all over the United States. These companies usually sell their products through a direct sales force; thus, the Ullmos' direct-response effort will be facing rather formidable competition. They understand this. They also understand that orders for ad specialty magnets come from a market that ranges from independent salespeople to huge organizations. The Ullmos believe that significant segments of the ad specialty magnet market still may not be well served, and some segments of it may not be served at all.

They further believe that the direct mail channel may be an ideal way to penetrate the unserved or poorly served portions of the ad specialty magnet market. They believe such market segments to include professionals such as lawyers, dentists, chiropractors, and financial planners (whose average order might be 1,000 or so ad specialty magnets per year) and also servicepeople such as plumbers and television technicians. Pizza parlors and similar food delivery or take-out operations, where customers order every other week or so, also seem to be an especially attractive market. High-ticket consumer goods dealerships also appear to include some attractive market segments.

The Ullmos have already had some success with a magnet promotional item while working with the dealers of a major tire company. In this case, the tire company sales manager encouraged his dealers (by inserting a letter in an S.E. Bennett mailing package to his dealers) to respond to an S.E. Bennett offer of emergency-number and ruler magnets.

The emergency-number magnets were very simple in concept, with a place on the magnet for fire, police, ambulance, physician, pharmacist, and other emergency numbers. Places for these numbers appeared directly under the word *EMERGENCY,*which was boldly printed at the top. The dealership name and logo and other information were placed directly under the emergency number blanks, taking up the remainder of the card.

The ruler magnets were simple business-card rulers and included dealership name and logo and other information.

This mailing to 3550 dealership salespeople produced 47 orders for ruler magnets and 95 orders for emergency-numbers magnets, a profitable 4 percent response rate.

The Self-Mailer

The format the Ullmos selected was a printed piece 8½ inches wide by 14 inches high that would fold twice to an 8½-inch-by-5½-inch self-mailer and incorporate a perforated 8½-inch-by-3-inch order card. The piece was to be printed on 105-pound Patina Matte dull-coated paper.

Cost estimates were as follows:

Two color—two sides

- 5,000 copies: $1,070
- 10,000 copies: $1,830
- 15,000 copies: $2,550

Four color—two sides

- 5,000 copies: $2,700
- 10,000 copies: $3,100
- 15,000 copies: $3,600

A local direct-response copy writer was contacted and agreed to create the self-mailer for $2500. This charge was to include concept development, copywriting, two photographs of the products in both black-and-white and color transparency format, an artist's layout for approval, and the finished art and typography.

Budget for Test Marketing

Tom and Jackie Ullmo are willing to spend in the neighborhood of $10,000 (beyond consultant fees) on this initial effort to sell ad specialty magnets by mail. They will proceed with the project or drop it depending on whether it still looks good after a direct marketing strategy is developed.

Questions

1. How good a fit is the ad specialty magnets product line for the direct-response channel?
2. What is the best list for the magnet ad specialty product line?
3. What is the best positioning for the magnet ad specialty product line?
4. Suggest an offer that should work with a selected list/market for the magnet ad specialty market. (This includes price, premium, guarantee, payment terms, time limits, etc.)
5. Select a format and layout for a direct mail package designed to sell magnet ad specialties to a selected market.
6. Sketch out a test marketing plan for selling promotional magnets to dentists.

The authors wish to gratefully acknowledge a contributing author, Nabil Hassan, Professor, Wright State University. Grateful appreciation is also extended to Tom and Jackie Ullmo for their cooperation and contribution to this case.

Direct Marketing Ethics

Direct marketing is not free from criticisms of the ethics of those practicing it. These concerns involve everything from the product to the promotion, distribution, and pricing of the product. Direct marketers must be concerned with the abuses by a small number of individuals and/or companies and must openly confront those whose ethics do not coincide with the high integrity of legitimate direct marketers.

The *Perfect Shaper* case provides good examples of many ethical concerns. The legitimacy and ethical practices regarding the product, the promotion literature, the distribution methods, and the pricing, are all a part of this case and can be explored in a cursory manner or in great depth. Either way, the reader is exposed to ethical decision making and the opportunity for abuse involved in direct marketing.

Case 19

Perfect Shaper
Selling a Dream by Mail

Over the past few years, many new companies have begun selling exercise and fitness equipment. Mark Brewer was a young fitness instructor with an entrepreneurial spirit; he had always been a natural at sales and was always looking for ways to make money. He had been involved in minor sales ventures since high school and had even made some money on a fishing gadget he invented when he was in college. When he saw the response of women to the fitness craze and realized that many of the women who were participating in his exercise classes were also buying exercise equipment for the abdomen and thighs, he thought of a way to take advantage of their interest. Mark knew this might be a fad and that there was much competition, but he believed there was quick money to be made. He was not bothered by the fact that he knew that these exercise products seldom accomplished what the buyer wanted because the buyer usually did not also eat correctly and was not disciplined sufficiently to use the product as much as it would have to be used to work; in fact, the amount of time needed to make a difference without also dieting was almost impossible for most people, and this was well known by fitness leaders such as Mark. Nevertheless, Mark reasoned that people still bought exercise products, so he might as well be the one to sell them and make money. With financing from his father and some of his father's friends (whom he later put on his board of directors) and help from an old college buddy, Gene Turner, who was in the plastics business, he developed a piece of equipment for tightening the abdominal muscles, similar to those already being sold successfully.

Mark called his equipment the Perfect Shaper. It was slightly different from the other products available, but generally it worked on the same principle as the others. The Perfect Shaper consisted of a spring positioned between two padded bars. The user would place the bars between her knees and shoulders and tone the abdominal, or stomach, muscles by doing a sit-up–like exercise against the resistance of the Perfect Shaper.

With a prototype of the product ready, Mark formed a business called Brewer Fitness, Inc. and went looking for a couple of people with good skills who would be interested in taking a chance on a new company. He hired a new college finance graduate, Ben Snyder, to manage the finances on a part-time basis. Because good jobs were scarce, Ben was willing to try to help Mark, with the understanding that he would reap the benefits if the product succeeded.

After forming the company, Mark set out to decide how best to promote the product. Mark had already planned to sell it through direct marketing, because he had used direct marketing to sell so many of his fishing gadgets. He could always put the product in stores later if the market lasted long enough. Mark was right, and the Perfect Shaper turned out to be an ideal product to offer through direct mail. The design and the features of the unique product could be explained in a graphical and detailed manner. This was preferable to having the product sit on a sporting-goods store shelf without any active selling. With direct mail sales increasing, many lists were available for targeting the Perfect Shaper to consumers who had bought similar types of equipment in the recent past.

Mark also decided to offer the product and see how many responses he would get before having the product produced. This was tricky because most people who order an exercise product want it right away; Mark decided not to indicate in the advertising how long it would take to deliver the product.

The key element of the direct mail package was a promotional video that showed the design of the Perfect Shaper and the benefits of using it regularly. Attractive models were utilized to present the product in a flattering way. Initially, there was concern that the video would be too expensive to create and reproduce; Mark knew, however, that the video would greatly enhance the likelihood of sales. To supplement the direct mail campaign, advertisements were placed in several exercise, health, and fitness magazines. The ads contained full-color pictures of models using the Perfect Shaper. An order form allowed the reader to either order the Perfect Shaper directly or to request the informational videocassette. Most of the responses were video requests.

Primarily due to Mark's knack for marketing and for selecting good direct mail lists, the Perfect Shaper caught on quickly as a method for firming up the stomach muscles. Within five weeks of putting out the first direct mail solo mailing to 1,000 names, Brewer Fitness, Inc. had orders for 216 Perfect Shapers. The magazine ads did not run until five months after his first list mailing, but they were as successful as the direct mail.

Mark quickly began thinking that he could produce other similar products for sale by direct mail, so it might pay him to have a small manufacturing plant of his own. He talked Gene Turner into becoming general manager of the plant as well as contributing some capital for a partnership. Within eight months, they had found a vacant building, purchased some basic equipment for producing the Perfect Shaper, and hired three people to work in the plant. They began producing Perfect Shapers on an as-needed basis. Fortunately, Gene was able to use suppliers whom he knew in the industry.

Sales for the Perfect Shaper increased steadily for three years. The third year's sales were further boosted by sales of Perfect Shaper accessories, including extra-cushioned bar pads and a storage bag. To assist with the marketing efforts, Meredith Lankster was hired as marketing manager. Unfortunately, the following year saw sales of the Perfect Shaper decline for the first year since its launch. Sales had peaked at 160,000 units, yet only 84,000 were sold during the past year.

Management Implications

With the approval of the board of directors, Mark Brewer hired a new president for the company. He realized that his strength was in organizing funding for and launching new ventures and marketing. Managing operations required special skills to ensure long-term success. He retained his position on the board of directors when Sharon Kane took over as president. Sharon had in the past started a small direct-mail company, which she later sold to a group of investors. Her expertise with direct-response marketing was the main consideration in hiring her as president of Brewer Fitness, Inc. because Mark wanted to work on other products in the future that could be sold by direct mail.

The new president immediately proved she brought diverse management skills to the company. She recognized that Brewer Fitness, Inc., was not fully utilizing its capacity. Sales must be increased, she thought, to take advantage of resources. In order to increase what she saw as a weak margin, Sharon began exploring options to control costs. The variable costs caught Sharon's immediate attention. While reviewing the firm's operations, she also focused attention on the marketing program that had been utilized to sell the Perfect Shaper and requested an analysis of the current marketing program from Meredith.

Marketing Proposal

Meredith was confident that the marketing program was sound. It had obviously brought initial success to Brewer Fitness. At this point, she concluded that in order to increase sales, the price of the Perfect Shaper would need to be lowered. The enthusiasts had already purchased the product, possibly regardless of price. The remainder of the market would need to be shown that the value of the product exceeded its price. Lowering the price would make this task more achievable.

Meredith proposed that the price of the Perfect Shaper be reduced by 25 percent, from $100 to $75. Because the market now could be expanded outside of exercise enthusiasts, Meredith also proposed moving advertising expenditures out of strictly health-related publications and into more broad-appeal magazines, including news and women's weeklies. The total outlay would not be changed, only the mix of magazines receiving the funds.

Sharon Kane was very interested in pursuing this option. She needed justification to do so, however. She asked Meredith to meet with Ben Snyder to analyze the numerical implications of this plan and to report back to her both the numbers and her subjective opinion on the proposed price change.

Financial Information

Ben Snyder suggested that Meredith and he start by determining the increased sales that would be necessary to reach the break-even point if the company followed Meredith's proposal. Costs would be divided into variable and fixed components as a first step to cost-volume-profit analysis. Pertinent costs to the analysis are listed in the following report:

Fixed costs and expenses:	
Manufacturing costs	$1,600,000
Marketing costs	200,000
Administrative and general costs	600,000
Total	$2,400,000

Variable costs and expenses:	
Manufacturing costs	$30
Marketing costs	10
Administrative and general costs	10
Total	$50

The next step for the two managers would be to calculate the amount of additional sales needed to break even. Then attention could be focused on the likelihood of producing that level of sales. Ben wrote down three guidelines, or assumptions, to direct their continued effort. These marketing assumptions were as follows:

1. Manufacturing capacity can support the increase in sales.
2. Costs associated with wages and materials are not expected to change for the foreseeable future.
3. The typical customer purchases $20 of accessories with the Perfect Shaper, and a resultant $5 in average variable costs is associated with these purchases.

Questions

1. What is Brewer Fitness, Inc.'s break-even point in dollars, assuming the company does not sell any of the accessories mentioned. Calculate break-even using both the old price of $100 and the new price of $75.

2. What is Brewer Fitness, Inc.'s break-even point in dollars, assuming the company does sell the amount of accessories mentioned in marketing assumption 3. Calculate break-even using both the old sales price of $100 and the new sales price of $75.

3. Determine the net additional Perfect Shaper sales necessary for Brewer Fitness, Inc. to break even under the proposed $75 selling price. Assume that no accessories are sold.

4. Determine the net additional Perfect Shaper sales necessary for Brewer Fitness to break even under the proposed $75 selling price assuming that accessories are sold as mentioned in assumption 3.

5. Determine the net income (or loss) for the following year if Brewer Fitness sells 84,000 Perfect Shapers. Calculate the net income (or loss) using both the old $100 selling price and the proposed $75 selling price. Assume that no accessories are sold.

6. Determine the maximum profit for the following year if Brewer Fitness returns to its previous sales peak and sells 160,000 Perfect Shapers without accessories. Assume that the price is $75 and that the company is operating at its current level.

7. Support the argument that price is driven by market value instead of accounting costs.

8. Explain what the market, cost, and competitive position would have to be for Meredith Lankster's proposal to work.

9. Discuss other strategies that you feel Meredith Lankster and Ben Snyder could propose to Sharon Kane, the president, as ways to increase sales and profits and why these would be successful.

10. Up to this point, administrative and general expenses have been included as variable costs. These costs were deducted from the selling price to determine the contribution margin, the contribution ratio, and the break-even points. Explain why you agree or disagree with this approach.

11. After much discussion and reflection, the principals in Brewer Fitness, Inc. began exploring the possibility of separating their enterprise into two separate legal entities: one a manufacturing company, to continue to be known as Brewer Fitness, Inc., and the other a marketing company, to be known as DirMar Marketing.

    This approach was designed to permit the manufacturing arm to be less fettered in its pursuit of making money through manufacturing and, likewise, for the marketing company to market with less regard for the needs of the manufacturing arm of the company.

For purposes of analysis, the principals assumed that Brewer Fitness, Inc., could profitably sell the Perfect Shaper to DirMar Marketing at $60 per unit in annual quantities ranging from 50 to 200,000 per year, and to continue selling at a profit of no more than 20 percent of variable cost and expenses if costs changed in the future. To analyze the viability of DirMar Marketing, it was decided to set up an electronic spreadsheet model of the company and test its profitability, assuming prices ranging from $75 to $125 per unit for the Perfect Shaper.

Response rates to direct response ads for exercise equipment and also ad costs in news and women's weeklies are based on readership. Preliminary investigation revealed that an ad costing approximately $10,000 can normally be used to reach approximately 333,333 readers. Based on their experience in the industry, the principals in this case assumed that DirMar Marketing ads would pull inquiries in a range from one-tenth to two-tenths of a percent of all readers, or from 333 to 666 responses for every $10,000 in ad costs. Other experience indicated that direct mail inquirers could be converted to buyers at a rate of approximately 2 buyers per 100 inquiries, or about 2 percent, with a range of from 1 to 3 buyers per 100 inquiries.

Using the data just presented, set up an electronic spreadsheet template that allows profit sensitivity analysis. See Exhibit 19-1 for an example of what might be done. Then vary the inputs to test the profitability of various assumed combinations of response rates, prices, ad costs, and other factors.

12. Did Mark Brewer violate the law by soliciting orders for the Perfect Shaper without telling his prospects that the product would not be produced unless enough orders were received?

13. Knowing as he did that 1) most people who buy exercise equipment don't use it for more than a few times after they buy it, and 2) exercise alone will not produce the results promised for the buyer of the Perfect Shaper, is Mark Brewer's selling of this product an act of unethical marketing?

The authors wish to gratefully acknowledge a contributing author, Nabil Hassan, Professor, Wright State University.

Exhibit 19-1   Sample Spreadsheet for Profit Sensitivity Analysis

Ad Cost = $10,000.00
Audience size = 333,333 readers

Response Rate (percent)	Total Inquiries	Units Sold Assuming 2 Percent Conversion	Sales at $100 per Unit	Cost of Goods Sold at $60 per Unit	Contribution per 333M Reached	Direct Profit per 333M Reached
0.100	333	16.65	$1,665	($666)	$2,331	($7,669)
0.200	666	33.30	$3,330	($1,332)	$4,662	($5,338)
0.300	999	49.95	$4,995	($1,998)	$6,993	($3,007)
0.400	1332	66.60	$6,660	($2,664)	$9,324	($676)
0.500	1665	83.25	$8,325	($3,330)	$11,655	$1,655
0.600	1998	99.90	$9,990	($3,996)	$13,986	$3,986
0.700	2331	116.55	$11,655	($4,662)	$16,317	$6,317
0.800	2664	133.20	$13,320	($5,328)	$18,648	$8,648
0.900	2997	149.85	$14,985	($5,994)	$20,979	$10,979
1.000	3330	166.50	$16,650	($6,660)	$23,310	$13,310
1.100	3663	183.15	$18,315	($7,326)	$25,641	$15,641
1.200	3996	199.80	$19,980	($7,992)	$27,972	$17,972
1.300	4329	216.45	$21,645	($8,658)	$30,303	$20,303
1.400	4662	233.10	$23,310	($9,324)	$32,634	$22,634
1.500	4995	249.75	$24,975	($9,990)	$34,965	$24,965
1.600	5328	266.40	$26,640	($10,656)	$37,296	$27,296
1.700	5661	283.05	$28,305	($11,322)	$39,627	$29,627
1.800	5994	299.70	$29,970	($11,988)	$41,958	$31,958
1.900	6327	316.35	$31,635	($12,654)	$44,289	$34,289
2.000	6660	333.00	$33,300	($13,320)	$46,620	$36,620
2.100	6993	349.65	$34,965	($13,986)	$48,951	$38,951
2.200	7326	366.30	$36,630	($14,652)	$51,282	$41,282
2.300	7659	382.95	$38,295	($15,318)	$53,613	$43,613
2.400	7992	399.60	$39,960	($15,984)	$55,944	$45,944
2.500	8325	416.25	$41,625	($16,650)	$58,275	$48,275
2.600	8658	432.90	$43,290	($17,316)	$60,606	$50,606

Marketing on the Internet

This section connects direct marketing to the emerging reality of direct marketing in the information age and the rapid advance of information technology during the last few years. Although advertising, as such, is not now tolerated on the Internet, it is clear that this nascent channel provides too much opportunity and too many potential marketing advantages to remain outside the direct marketing arena for very long. *OIA, Inc.* is an important precursor of things to come as it challenges readers to consider the probable shape of Internet advertising designed to benefit all while harming no one. This case represents truly groundbreaking direct marketing.

Case 20

OIA, Inc.

An Agency Considers Advertising on the Internet

OIA, Inc., is a modest-sized business-to-business advertising agency that has been in business since 1949. The firm's traditional business was the preparation and implementation of marketing communication plans for clients who wanted advertisements placed in business or trade publications (60 percent of agency revenue) and preparation of sales literature (40 percent of agency revenue). OIA's clientele was regional, with new business generated largely by direct mailings and personal sales calls. The agency's historically solid billings began to soften in the early 1990s with the downsizing of companies and an accompanying decline in business and trade magazine advertising.

In response to this, OIA began considering a change in its offerings to include the writing of technical manuals and interactive video productions. "Both of these capabilities have been stripped out of downsized companies, and that's creating a big demand," said Rick Boden, OIA's general manager. OIA tested this idea by listing its technical writing service in *Thomas Register of American Manufacturers*. The results were dramatic. Within six months of publication, OIA had received ten qualified inquiries that ultimately led to the landing of two large clients.

In view of this success, Warren Rogers, president of OIA, proposed that OIA investigate advertising on the emerging Internet. Rogers observed, "Millions of people access the Internet. They communicate their problems and offer solutions to each other, often obtaining information in minutes or hours versus weeks or months the old way. We might be able to use the Internet to find fast answers to our own problems." Rick Boden agreed with the potential but expressed a valid and widespread reservation when he said, "Companies that try blatant advertising on the Internet get flamed—buried in derisive junk messages. It's a swift way to get a bad reputation."

"That's a possibility," said Rogers, "but I think we can make it work if we understand and reflect some marketing and interactive communication basics in our planning." Rogers explained that true interactive marketing is driven by the buyer's problem, not the seller's problem. "There are more prospects out there trying to find us and what we offer than we're finding. We need to discover these prospects, qualify them, and make offers to them. Our problem is to find them, but to do so will require that we facilitate their search for the solutions we offer. The view that interactive marketing is essentially what happens when rotating jewelry and an 800 number are displayed on television is wrong," he said. "That view misses the point that interactive marketing is two-way communication, not a one-way dump of the seller's information."

With that, Rogers commissioned Boden to proceed. "Don't be blatant," he said. "I think your best approach is most likely to be putting some questions and answers out that will attract people with problems we can solve. This should work, and not be blatant advertising, if we can include a few questions and answers that will help prospects qualify OIA as a potential problem solver. This approach has worked for some of our clients; why shouldn't it work for us? As you know, the question-and-answer approach is the heart of special interest groups, forums, and bulletin boards. Maybe you can just offer additional information to people who have the kinds of problems we're seeking to solve," said Rogers.

Questions

Investigate the current state of marketing on the Internet and help Mr. Boden answer the following questions:

1. Was it wise for OIA to try to find a way to advertise its services over the Internet?
2. Was Warren Rogers accurate when he said that interactive marketing must be based on the buyer's problem rather than the seller's problem?
3. What kinds of questions and answers might attract prospects seeking solutions in the form of OIA's service offerings? What questions might prospects want answered by OIA? What questions might OIA want answered to qualify interested prospects?
4. What ethical problems are being raised by his boss's insistence that OIA advertise on the Internet, given Boden's reluctance?
5. Would it be better for OIA to expand its listing and place ads in *Thomas Register* before trying other media? After all, *Thomas Register* had produced good results.
6. Frame and answer at least three additional questions of your own—questions that will provide guidance for OIA as it investigates and/or develops its Internet marketing program.

This case was prepared by Roger W. Brucker, Odiorne Industrial Advertising.

International Direct Marketing Cases

It is essential that the international aspect of direct marketing be explored in some depth since it is likely to be a major growth area for companies in the future. Direct marketing internationally is not new, of course, but it is an area of great interest and increased participation for more and more companies.

One of the issues of greatest concern for international direct marketing involves the viability of the product for different cultures and the viability of direct marketing for selling that product to these different cultures. *McLean Originals* is a wonderful example of these concerns and of a company attempting to market directly to United States businesses and individual consumers.

The remaining two cases in this section are very real illustrations of the enormous complexities and conflicts involved with the interaction among channels of distribution on an international scale. *Trident Sports, Inc.* represents an American company expanding internationally, and *Oriflame* represents a European company expanding internationally and into the United States.

Case 21

Trident Sports, Inc.
An International Seller Looks for Leads

Trident Sports, Inc., is a six-year-old company headquartered in Dayton, Ohio. The firm was founded by Gilles de Courtivron and Allen Byrum as an international trading company and distributor, specializing in the export of "Made in America" or "Designed in America" sporting goods and leisure products.

Both Gilles and Allen had extensive previous international marketing experience when they launched Trident Sports. Gilles had spent 25 years as an international marketing manager at NCR Corporation World Headquarters in Dayton and also worked for many years at NCR France in Paris. Allen's experience included 15 years as marketing manager for Harris Printing Corporation in Latin America and then some time in a similar role with BOMAG Co., a German manufacturer of civil engineering equipment. Shortly after their retirements and after considerable exploration, Gilles and Allen concluded that, considering industry data and their backgrounds, exporting sporting goods and leisure products of American manufacture offered them the business opportunity for which they had been looking. Their research on France, a market well known to Gilles, showed particular promise, especially for all-terrain bicycles, most often called mountain bikes, together with parts and components for this sport.

Road cycling, a sport mainly engaged in by French men, had been very popular in France for many years. However, the popularity of the sport among women and as a family togetherness activity was growing rapidly. Considerable consumer disposable income is a requirement for the typical participant in the sport; therefore, sales opportunities were thought to be best in the most developed countries, including the Netherlands, the United Kingdom, France, Switzerland, Spain, Sweden, Japan, and Canada. Accordingly, Trident chose to prospect these countries first, with a plan to move in the near future to smaller countries such as Austria, New Zealand, Finland, Norway, and Morocco.

In 1988, the partners test-marketed various brands of high-grade and expensive hand-made U.S. mountain bikes directly to dealers in France through an agent. The results of this test strongly suggested that the French market was not ready to accept the high prices demanded by top-of-the-line American bike makers. As a result, Trident decided to discontinue the sale of complete bikes and focused all of their efforts on the export of cycle parts, components, and accessories. This led, in 1990, to formation of a joint venture with a former international manager of Peugeot Cycles, the largest bicycle maker in France, for the purpose of distributing bicycle parts and components in that country. This new venture is located in Paris and employs six salesmen who cover the French market, calling principally on specialty bike shops.

In 1992, Trident Sports increased the range of its product line by adding sport or stunt kites. Camping goods, sportswear, and kayaks were added in 1993, the same year the company began to venture out to countries other than France. Today, Trident has customers in Canada, the United Kingdom, France, Switzerland, Austria, Spain, Japan, New Zealand, Australia, Ireland, Norway, Sweden, and Morocco. Trident also sells a line of German-made bottom brackets to bicycle makers in the United States and Canada and also to the wholesalers who service the bicycle aftermarket in both countries. All current products sold by Trident Sports are of the highest quality, and neither de Courtivron nor Byrum will compromise quality on any product their company handles.

Current Trident Product Line

Bicycle products sold by Trident are state-of-the-art in technology, design, engineering, and materials—all important issues in a sport in which performance is greatly increased by well-designed, very strong and lightweight parts. Typical of the high-performance bicycle components sold by Trident are bottom brackets, cranksets, pedals, handlebars and bar ends, grips, composite wheels, wheel rims, brake pads, hubs and spokes, and seatposts. These are usually made from advanced composite materials and exotic metals such as carbon fiber and titanium. Approximately 30 well-known U.S. manufacturers of such parts are represented by Trident Sports in its various overseas markets.

Six brands of kayaks are sold by Trident. Two of these, both of which are made of high-grade crosslink plastics and which are stronger than other boats offered by U.S. kayak makers, are consistent winners in world-class competition. Trident's camping equipment is made by major American manufacturers of tents, sleeping bags, stoves, and lanterns. Sometimes these products are designed in the United States but manufactured in other countries such as Mexico, Brazil, and several Asian countries. Trident also sells top-quality U.S.-made sportswear such as t-shirts and sweatshirts that have contemporary outdoor and marine designs.

In early 1993, Trident became general agent for North America for KSS Precision Company of Schweinfurt, Germany, a manufacturer of high-quality but competitively priced sealed-bottom brackets. Major OEM (original equipment manufacturer) sales of these brackets were made to large North American companies such as Trek, Cannondale, Rocky Mountain Bicycles, and KONA. KSS sales in six-digit quantities are expected for 1995 models. The year 1994 also marked the beginning of KSS sales to the bicycle aftermarket in the United States and Canada.

Channels of Distribution

The principal channel of distribution for bicycle parts of the type Trident sells are small, specialized, and sometimes very tiny bike shops. Japan has about 34,000 such shops. France has about 7,000, approximately the same number as are in the United States. Trident's sporting goods and leisure products have much wider distribution because many other types of stores carry them, including department stores and sporting goods stores. Trident Sports sells only to importers and distributors in each country who can purchase volume quantities and import directly from Trident. Normally, the company does not sell directly to retailers except in the case of chain store organizations and large department stores. A minimum purchase amount of $500 per order is required.

Promotion

In early 1993, the company began advertising its sport kites in *Commercial News USA,* a catalog of new products published by the United States Department of Commerce. This effort generated 75 responses from various parts of the world but only one, a Japanese importer, materialized into a large customer for Trident Sports. Efforts are currently underway to obtain wider exposure and coverage by participating in catalog trade shows sponsored by the Department of Commerce. These shows are conducted in many countries and are a major distribution channel for the product catalogs of U.S. exporting firms. Interested importers write directly to the U.S. firm for additional information. Leads at these shows equal about 4 percent of total visitors. Across all participating companies, these are converted to sales at a rate estimated to range from 1 to 2 percent of visitors.

Most of Trident's products appear to get excellent consumer ratings, but sales have been restrained, especially on some products. This is thought to be largely the result of high import duties on U.S. products across all countries in the European Economic Union (in some cases as much as 20 percent), and thus, to generally higher prices for Trident products than for those of head-to-head competitors.

Despite this disadvantage, Trident Sports' total sales for 1994 were projected to reach approximately $1 million. The firm's mid-1994 sales were broken down as follows:

Bicycle products	60 percent
Sport kites	10 percent
Bottom brackets	10 percent
Camping equipment	10 percent
Kayaks	5 percent
Sportswear	5 percent

The firm's only full-time employees are its two partners. The company operates with its customers on a cost-plus basis and its margins come from a service fee of 10.0 to 12.5 percent added on to Trident Sports' cost of goods in each order. Net profit before tax is about 5 percent of total sales. Customers are responsible for paying all freight costs from Dayton to the final destination.

Method of Operation

Trident is dedicated to providing high-quality services to its customers and has developed a unique method of operation that is fast and efficient and offers savings to its customers. The company offers products that are made by approximately 40 to 50 different suppliers located all over the United States.

Trident's method of operation offers its customers the following significant advantages:

- *Savings on communications*: A single order to Trident replaces the many orders that would have to be sent to many different factories.
- *Savings on freight rates*: All orders are consolidated in Dayton and the goods are shipped from the factories to the Trident warehouse by inexpensive land transportation (normally UPS). Ninety percent of orders are shipped to the overseas destination by air freight. Only 10 percent of sales go by surface freight—sea container and LCL (less than carload) shipments. Freight carriers apply shipping charges by volume or by dimensional weight and invoice, whichever is the highest. In order to optimize these charges, Trident repackages each factory's shipping carton in order to eliminate any empty space that would add to the shipping costs. This is labor-intensive work, but it saves the customers a substantial amount of money on high international freight charges.
- *Savings on landed costs*: At the destination, fixed charges are invoiced to the consignee by freight forwarders for receiving and delivering the shipment and by customs brokers for clearing each

shipment of goods with the customs authorities. These are substantial charges that can reach several hundred dollars per shipment. A single consolidated shipment from Trident reduces these charges significantly.

- *Ease of payment of U.S. suppliers' merchandise invoices:* Because the factories are located in many parts of the United States, the goods for consolidated shipment reach Dayton at different times. Normally, orders for five or six different factories are placed on the same day. The goods for a complete shipment are received by Trident Sports within a two-to-three-week period. In most cases, a U.S. supplier requires advance cash payment for each shipment of goods going to an overseas destination. The alternative is to arrange payment by a bank's letter of credit (LC). LCs are expensive and often inflexible and cumbersome.

To make it easier and less expensive for the customer, Trident pays U.S. suppliers directly from its own bank account from Dayton. These sales are handled by the factories as standard U.S. domestic transactions, which usually have terms of payment at 30 days of invoice. In six years of operations, no payment has been made by Trident to any supplier past its invoice due date; therefore, the company's payment reliability is well established.

The overseas customer pays Trident by wire transfer upon advice that the goods are ready for shipment. This advice is given by way of a faxed pro forma invoice usually sent on the shipping date. A regular invoice accompanies the merchandise. As a result, Trident receives the customer's funds several weeks or days before the suppliers' invoices are due. Certain precautions are taken when purchases are made by new customers. Trident has encountered virtually no payment problems with its overseas customers. Most goods are invoiced FOB Dayton, Ohio.

Future Plans

For the next three years, it is expected that significant growth will come from sales of kayaks, sportswear, and camping equipment. Sales in these categories are expected to increase by approximately 20 to 25 percent each year, and bicycle products are expected to show smaller increases. New lines will be added as related export opportunities are identified.

Questions

1. Describe what appears to be the business mission of Trident Sports. Do you think its owners have a business vision? Write out

a brief mission or vision statement that appears to be viable for the company, given its markets, products, and resources.

2. What direct-response marketing techniques does Trident Sports already appear to be using?

3. Evaluate the potential of using direct response techniques to "push" the Trident product line through its distribution channel and to "pull" the Trident product line through its distribution channel.

4. What are the elements of a direct-response program that will work for Trident Sports while blending into its overall marketing program? Sketch out the structure of such a program.

5. Assume that Trident decides to pursue a "push" strategy and that generating leads among agents and distributors in its target countries is necessary. What creative/positioning concept do you think is needed? Identify at least three positioning concepts that appear to have merit. Outline a method for qualifying "push" leads.

6. Assume that Trident decides to pursue a "pull" strategy and that generating leads among retail dealers in its target countries is necessary. What creative/positioning concept do you think is needed? Identify at least three positioning concepts that appear to have merit. Outline a method for qualifying "pull" leads.

7. Do you think it is necessary for personnel to be fluent in a country's language before a firm can successfully direct market there?

8. Check with your phone-service provider to determine if 800 numbers can be set up to receive responses by phone directly from foreign countries, and also what it costs to make a typical call to at least three foreign countries.

9. Check with your local postal service to determine the cost of mailing to and receiving mail from at least three foreign countries.

10. Describe any inherent weaknesses in the operating methods of Trident Sports that would cause the company to become especially vulnerable in the near future?

11. What marketing methods would optimize Trident's profits over the short term?

12. From the business strategy viewpoint, are sporting goods and leisure products sales in industrially developed countries sustainable quality markets for the visible future? Why or why not?

13. What commercial or promotional actions should Trident Sports initiate to trigger faster, more profitable growth and development?

The authors wish to gratefully acknowledge a contributing author, Gilles de Courtivron, Owner, Trident Associates.

Case 22   Oriflame

Expanding International Direct, Distributor, and Mail Order Sales

Oriflame International S.A. (OISA), Luxembourg, was established in 1972. It includes a group of companies associated in a variety of ways, now referred to collectively as the Group. The conglomerate currently sells in 41 countries, including countries in Europe, the Far East, Australia, and the Americas.

In 1987, Oriflame introduced the Vevay brand name, expanded its mail-order operation, made Fleur de Santé, a natural cosmetics company, an associate of the group, and acquired Hallbergs, the oldest and second-largest jewelry store chain in Sweden.

ACO Hud was acquired in 1992, adding Sweden's best-known brand name in skin care to the company's stable of products. These products are retailed through Swedish, Norwegian, and Icelandic pharmacies. Oriflame now develops and produces its own naturally based skin-care products in its manufacturing plant in Ireland, where the Group's research laboratories are also located.

Oriflame Eastern Europe S.A. (ORESA), which is managed from Brussels and 25 percent owned by OISA, was established in 1990 to penetrate eastern European markets. ORESA holds a license to sell Oriflame's products in eastern Europe and certain other countries.

Oriflame uses direct selling in 39 of its target market countries. Direct selling accounted for 61 percent of the Group's sales. Thirteen of the direct sales companies, mostly in Europe, are wholly owned. Associate companies operate in 13 additional countries. The main associated company is Oriflame Eastern Europe (ORESA), in which OISA has a 25 percent interest. Oriflame also has licensees operating in 13 other countries.

Oriflame's products are manufactured in modern facilities on the outskirts of Dublin, Ireland. All products undergo strict physical, chemical, and microbiological control before reaching the customer. The objective is to ensure that the customer can rely on Oriflame products to provide long-term quality, regardless of how they are purchased.

The Market

The global market for cosmetics and toiletries (C&T) is in a mature life-cycle stage, but is still averaging around 4 percent annual growth per year. Growth decreased in 1992 and 1993 as a consequence of the economic recession that affected most of the world. Market participants are under constant pressure for innovation and operate with low levels of legal protection surrounding their patents. However, given its 3 percent annual growth projections through the year 2000, cosmetics and toiletries is still an attractive market. The European C&T market accounts for 37 percent of world C&T sales and is the world's largest single market for C&T products. Europe's 1992 C&T growth rate of 8 percent is among the strongest of any in the world, especially when the results from eastern Europe are considered.

C&T cosmetic sales in Europe are geographically spread as follows: Sweden (20 percent), United Kingdom (15 percent), Finland (13 percent), Denmark (11 percent), Eastern Europe (11 percent), Spain (7 percent), Holland (6 percent), Norway (4 percent), other (13 percent).

Oriflame has a very extensive C&T product line, covering most of the entire family's needs. The company also markets beauty-enhancing products such as fashion jewelry, related accessories, and health foods. All are marketed using both direct sales and direct marketing methods.

Skin care is a large sector of the C&T market in most countries. Europe's skin-care market is more developed than its counterpart in the United States. Key trends across the entire skin care market include increasing sophistication of buyers and the development and positioning of products as offering health or therapeutic benefits. These products, called "cosmeceuticals," are expected to become a major growth area in the skin-care market. Recently, the cosmetics industry has been the focus of intensive product research and development as well as aggressive efforts to transfer medical research findings into cosmetic products.

The highest growth in skin care continues to be in the area of anti-aging products. Consumer demand for quality is rising on long-lasting moisturizer products. In addition, the public's concern about environmental pollution and the link to the harmful effect of the sun's ultraviolet rays are of increasing interest to the industry and a promising source of future growth. Body-care products also sell well in Europe, but market penetration levels are relatively low compared to the sun-care market.

The direct sales channel for cosmetics and skin-care products accounts for 10 to 15 percent of the global cosmetics market. Oriflame is one of the largest direct sales companies in many of its markets, and is, overall, the largest direct sales company in Scandinavia. Direct sales accounted for 61 percent of Oriflame's total company sales in 1994, up from 58 percent in 1993.

The Direct Selling Industry

Direct selling, which was already a substantial industry in the United States by the 1920s, is defined by the Direct Selling Association as follows:

> The selling of consumer goods direct to private individuals, in their homes and places of work, through transactions initiated and concluded by salespersons. Direct selling has several advantages over shop retailing, not only for the customer, but also for the manufacturer. The customer can pick up the products at a service center or have them delivered to their home. The manufacturer does not have to support advertising cost to attract its customers. The distributors play a double role—being both customers and salespeople—to recruit new customers.

The World Federation of Direct Selling Associations indicated that direct selling was a $60 billion world industry in 1994, with 15 million people involved. The United States alone had 5 to 7 million people in direct selling; Japan accounted for more than 2 million. People who perform direct selling activities of course want to increase their incomes, but another and possibly more important motivation is the opportunity that direct selling provides for them to be independent of organizational constraints common to most jobs.

The steady growth in Oriflame's sales, which started in 1982, continued into 1994, when sales reached $105 million. The company's direct sales channel sales growth has been particularly significant in Europe. The company believes this to be the result of people's becoming more discerning about how they buy things and a trend back to personal service, care, and attention. These factors, combined with Oriflame's commitment to offering value for money and a full 100 percent money-back guarantee, appear to explain Oriflame's recent success in Europe. Major company growth has also been experienced in South and Central America, including Chile, the country from which Oriflame's operations in South America are directed. Sales growth for Oriflame's associated company, ORESA, which started in 1990, have also been impressive, with 1994 sales to licensees increasing by 41 percent over the preceding year.

Oriflame's Selling Methods

The Direct Selling Operation

Oriflame products are sold by independent distributors (not employed by Oriflame) directly to the customer. Each distributor works independently and develops his or her own organization. Oriflame does research, develops and packages the product, and handles financing and data processing, warehousing, shipping, and marketing, and also creates training programs and materials in support of their distributors.

When conventional selling is used for C&T products, the product moves through a hierarchy of middlemen from the manufacturer to the end customer. All of these intermediaries earn a profit from handling the product. Using the direct sales approach, intermediary functions and profits are shared among the distributors. The cost reductions that result give Oriflame the capability to sell a higher-quality product at lower and much more competitive prices than can normally be found at retail.

The Oriflame distributors offer unique value-added services such as cosmetic consulting in their customers' homes or offices. It is company policy that prospective customers of distributors 1) are not subjected to pressure selling or made to feel that they are obliged to purchase, 2) receive free skin analysis and personalized advice on proper skin care, and 3) are offered free ongoing after-sales service.

Oriflame has 250,000 consultants worldwide. Consultants usually have other jobs; thus, their involvement with Oriflame is sometimes only a hobby. Historically, consultants have been paid strictly on commission and their primary sales tool has been sales catalogs provided by Oriflame. (More than 12 million catalogs in 17 languages are distributed by Oriflame every year.) Consultants get their catalogs every two, three, or four weeks and use them to sell to friends, relatives, and colleagues—normally their primary customer base. Consultants order products they sell from the catalogs, receive bundled shipments from Oriflame, and then pass the products on to individual customers.

Oriflame is now testing and expanding a new marketing method. This involves the consultant's building up a sales network and receiving a bonus or commission on the sales made by each individual recruited to be a distributor, as well as on her or his own sales. This system, often called multilevel marketing, can offer career opportunities for current "hobbyists" because the system permits "main-source" levels of income. The method has worked most successfully for Oriflame in Latin America and several eastern European countries. Consultants in these countries often enjoy incomes well above the national average. Catalogs are an integral part of this system, but are issued less frequently. Oriflame is now adapting this method for use in its traditional western European markets.

Mail Order: Vevay and Fleur de Santé brand names

Oriflame's mail-order operation was started in Denmark in 1978. The program now includes Oriflame's cosmetics club in Denmark, which now has about 100,000 members and sales of nearly $11 million; Vevay's cosmetics club, founded in Sweden in 1987, with about 180,000 members and sales of $6.6 million; and Fleur de Santé.

Fleur de Santé has been an associated company of OISA since May 1992. In September 1992, OISA acquired an additional 6 percent, increasing its ownership to 36 percent. It sells natural cosmetics directly to the customer via mail order. The company, which is located in Malmö, has a volume of about $20 million in Sweden, Norway, and Finland. In August 1992, OISA acquired the distribution rights for Fleur de Santé in eastern Europe. A new associated company was started in the Czech Republic in February 1993.

Oriflame and Vevay sell natural-ingredients–based cosmetics via mail order using a book-club type of system. Buyers join cosmetics clubs and receive cosmetics shipments through the mail 10 to 12 times a year. Member prices are highly competitive, partly due to the use of less elaborate packaging than that used for similar products sold through normal retail stores. The cosmetics package the members will receive is presented to them in the catalog and then delivered automatically unless the customer notifies the company to the contrary.

Fleur de Santé sells about 250 different natural cosmetics items via mail order. The catalogs are distributed 12 to 15 times a year. In the Czech Republic, Fleur de Santé products are sold using the party-plan concept. Sales increased by 7 percent last year to $22 million. Growth has been less than in previous years because of the recession in Europe. Oriflame and Vevay in Denmark increased by 13 percent and 50 percent respectively. Sales in France and the United Kingdom, however, ceased as a consequence of a decision to close the Vevay business in these markets. Sales to associate Fleur de Santé, Sweden, increased by 18 percent.

Mail order in 1994 accounted for 13 percent of total Oriflame sales.

	1994	1993
Sales (in thousands)	$23,176	$22,254
Capital expenditures (in thousands)	$80	$48
Number of employees	58	48
Number of club members	400,000	417,000
Number of Countries	9	9

Hallberg's and ACO

Oriflame departed from its core distribution method, direct selling, in 1987, when it acquired Hallberg's, a jewelry company, and ACO, a company that markets skin-care products through pharmacies.

Hallberg's, whose head office is located in Malmö, is Sweden's oldest jewelry company and currently has 31 stores throughout the country. The company was founded in 1860 by Carl-Gustaf Hallberg and has been a leading manufacturer and jewelry store chain since the early part of the 20th century. Hallberg's product focus is high-quality jewelry, gift articles, and silver cutlery. Today, the company has sales of around $24 million, about 7 percent of the market.

Oriflame is moving to reduce the number of small Hallberg stores and concentrate on large stores in major Swedish cities. This, together with the introduction of a franchise concept during 1993, is designed to provide a base for future growth.

In 1992, Oriflame made another acquisition: ACO, a marketer of creams, lotions, and sun-care and hand-care products. ACO's main market is Sweden; its distribution there is through pharmacies. ACO is the best-known brand name for skin-care products in Sweden. Its products are in the low and average price ranges, and its recent sales growth has come mainly from newly introduced products and from established sun-care products. Sales increased to $24 million in 1993.

In 1994, the Oriflame Group results were as follows:

	1994	1993
Sales (000)	173,472	167,134
Operation profit	25,194	23,508
Profit before tax	27,946	23,878
Profit after tax	23,712	21,034
Capital expenditure	6,588	11,000
Profit margin (percent)	16.1	14.3
Equity/assets ratio	57.3	43.9
Return on net capital employed (percent)	31.0	33.0
Gearing (percent)	10.0	22.0
Number of employees	858	798

Key Factors in Oriflame's Success

Looking back through the years, it appears that four factors have been key to Oriflame's success to date.

1. From the beginning, Oriflame used a local management policy. Expatriates were never sent to a country, even those with a solid knowledge and experience of the company's products and culture. In each country, the company placed ads in the newspapers to recruit local managers and staff. Recruiters spent much time in interviews to explain the nature and spirit of a free-market economy, the direct selling method, and the Oriflame marketing plan to potential new staff.

2. The marketing plan itself was considered the main asset of the company. Headquarters supplied ample support, guidance, and training to help local markets. The marketing plan, called "The Success Plan," was the same for each country but had minor adaptation whenever needed.
3. Public relations has always been handled well; explaining the direct selling method very clearly has always been considered a necessity.
4. Maintaining high product quality has also always been a requirement. To ensure this, the company has always manufactured about 65 percent of its 165 products itself and required that these and all other products be made from pure, natural ingredients.

Questions

1. Critique Oriflame's overall marketing strategy. Describe its strengths and weaknesses. Then take on the role of adviser to the management of Oriflame and help the company decide which markets to pursue and how to improve its approach to its markets.
2. Define and address the problems and opportunities that would accompany a decision to expand into additional new markets, particularly into the United States, using direct marketing as the primary distribution strategy.
3. Design a test mail-order marketing strategy for entering the U.S. market.

This case was prepared by Dominique Xardel, Graduate School of Management, ESSEC, Cergy-Pointoise, France.

Case 23   McLean Originals
Assessing the Viability of Selling Dolls by Mail

Jan McLean Originals is a small business in Dunedin, a small city on the South Island of New Zealand. The business has recently grown rapidly by successfully producing limited-edition porcelain dolls for collectors. Jan's dolls have had a big impact on the American doll collector's circuit during the last three years. There is now a long waiting list for her products at good prices, and Jan can hardly believe her success and her good fortune. She now faces a number of decisions concerning her rapidly growing business. She is keen to explore the European and Japanese markets because she feels the American market is nearing maturity. She intends to visit Germany and experience some of the traditional toy-making factories. She is also considering the production of designer teddy bears, the latest rage in collectibles overseas, and selling them with her established label. Yet another option would be for Jan to move operations closer to her main markets where she would be closer to many of the raw materials needed.

Doll making and collecting is an ancient tradition in many parts of the world. The Egyptian, Greek and Roman Empires all had dolls—usually as religious accessories rather than playthings. In the seventeenth century, wooden Scandinavian, Austrian, and German dolls were produced as children's toys. Porcelain dolls were first introduced into the American market in the nineteenth century. Old dolls are much sought after and fetch a high price on the collectors' markets.

Doll making and collecting is now a very big industry. Currently in the United States dolls are the number-one collectable, being even more popular than stamps. Jan McLean Originals, after taking the doll collecting community in America by storm in 1991, are currently in high demand. Jan is now a world-acclaimed doll maker and artist, but is modest about her success.

When interviewed about her business success, Jan explained, "A lot of things made it easier for me when I started out in the doll business. I was 40 years old—when you get to your 40s you don't care anymore about what people think. I had a husband who could look after the kids. I was financially independent. And I had the example of my parents who were both business people."

Jan was trained and worked as a nurse in Dunedin for 23 years and initially began making and painting pottery as a hobby in the 1970s. She made her first doll in 1983 and in the same year enrolled in a doll making course and made and hand-painted two porcelain doll reproductions. Her interest and experience in doll-making grew, and in the following year she and her sister opened a commercial ceramics studio with only NZ$2,000 in cash and NZ$5,000 mortgage each. They bought machines and equipment and recruited and trained staff to produce and sell porcelain doll heads, components, and molds. They worked regularly from 9 A.M. to 11 P.M., seven days a week. Jan also worked as a nurse at night. After two years they decided to sell this business. Despite the long hours of work and the commitment they made to the business, it was not providing sufficient reward or personal satisfaction. It was sold for NZ$100,000.

In the following years Jan continued to produce and hand-paint dolls as well as conduct doll making classes. In 1990 an American businessman visiting Dunedin saw the dolls and was very enthusiastic about their design and quality. His wife was a keen collector of porcelain dolls. He suggested that Jan should exhibit her dolls at the 1991 Trade-Only American International Toy Fair in New York. About the same time a Singaporean telephoned to order a custom-made doll and also recommended that she exhibit at the Toy Fair in New York. The cost of the booth at the Toy Fair—US$3,500—was a deterrent, but Jan decided to book an exhibitor's stand after borrowing the required financing from her mother.

Jan rates the Toy Fair as the most exciting thing to ever happen to her. She arrived at the Fair without any promotional material or order books and had to put a tablecloth on the display stand to show her dolls. The stand was soon crowded with visitors and potential customers, and the pressure was continuous for several days. She sold her 23 dolls in the first hour of setting up the display and later returned to New Zealand with US$40,000 from the sales. She also met agents, who gave her enough orders to keep her busy for several years.

Jan then turned her home into a porcelain doll studio and factory and was encouraged in this by a supportive family. The business grew in strength from its small beginnings as a cottage industry, and the sales turnover grew to over NZ$500,000 in the next two years. Since then, Jan McLean Originals has flourished into a thriving export business with rapidly increasing sales approaching NZ$1 million. Jan McLean Originals now employs 7 people and occupies factory premises in South Dunedin, which is an industrial area in the city. Jan describes the atmosphere at the factory as relaxed but focused. She also employs 13 outworkers who work on a contract basis making accessories such as shoes, hats, wigs, and jewelry and the occasional pieces of furniture to go with her limited edition dolls. Most of these accessories are designed by Jan to complement her dolls. Other furniture and accessories come from Indonesia, where Jan buys each piece cheaply and further refines them to increase their quality and presentability. She deals with representatives in Indonesia who are familiar with her products and her requirements.

Sales and Marketing

There are four types of dolls produced and sold worldwide. *One-of-a-kind* and *limited-edition* dolls are designed and made by a doll artist for the top end of the market. *Vinyl dolls* made in Asia, Germany and Spain are priced between US$395–US$800. *Mass-produced porcelain dolls*, in Asia, are generally small, from 12 to 14 inches in height, and priced from US$30–US$300.

Jan specializes in limited-edition and "one-of-a-kind" dolls of up to 48 inches in height. They have names such as Pansy, Poppy, Primrose, and Marigold. Keen collectors like to have a whole series of dolls in their collections. Current market price for a limited-edition doll (normally produced in runs of 100 or less) is about US$2,500. A one-of-a-kind doll can sell for US$15,000. Some doll makers can sell them for up to US$48,000. Jan also makes "small edition" dolls (limited to 10) and sells them for US$7,500 each. In total, Jan McLean Originals now sells 400 dolls per year to the lucrative American market, 15 to the Australian market at an annual show in Sydney, and only 15 to the New Zealand market. The dolls are not promoted or actively sold in shops locally, and the few sales in New Zealand are made to collectors who make a direct contact with the company.

Each doll is very labor-intensive, with only eight to ten made per week. Most of these are "limited-edition" dolls with only about five percent "small" edition or one-of-a-kind. Jan believes that a doll can be hand-made and painted for a minimum of NZ$800 in New Zealand while in Asia it could be mass produced for NZ$35. However, the Asian-produced doll would be of a much lower quality, particularly in the painting.

Jan McLean Originals now sells through 25 American dealers and is gaining exposure through annual visits to the New York Toy Fair, where many dealers place their orders for the year. After the Fair, orders are received and confirmed by fax. Jan has to allocate a certain number of dolls to each dealer because some dealers order large numbers in order to starve other dealers of her dolls. However, Jan plans to alleviate this by requiring a deposit for each doll ordered. Dealers and sales agents advertise and promote her dolls, allowing her time to concentrate on making very high-quality products, and she spares no expense in making them. Jan is able to boast a number of famous business people and celebrities as customers including film star Demi Moore, author Ann Rice and singer Marie Osmond. Many other doll collectors buy Jan's dolls, both because of their appreciation of the high levels of quality craftsmanship that make the dolls so distinctive, and also as an investment. Each edition is documented and the slip-cast mold, which is unique for each edition, is destroyed once the production run is completed. Some of her dolls have been sold for more than three times their original price.

The estimated size of the market open to Jan remains relatively unestablished, but the potential market in the USA is immense. Selling 400 dolls each year in the United States is only the tip of the iceberg.

Competition is also very high. However, the quality and presentation of Jan's dolls make them highly distinctive and sought after in comparison to most other dolls. "I'm at one end of the market," says Jan. "I do limited editions of dolls that are 32 inches high. If I wanted, I could reproduce the dolls for another part of the market, either in vinyl, a different size, or different quality. I could do this, and I'd sell millions all over America, but I choose not to. I try to remain 'elusive and exclusive.'"

By targeting this particular market niche, Jan is able to keep her business at a controllable and personal level, and by 'drip feeding' the market, she has made her dolls highly sought-after collectable items.

Payment for the dolls is arranged before the finished doll is sent to the customer. This is done through telegraphic transfer, credit card or personal check. With credit card authorization or checks sent in advance, Jan receives full payment, avoiding any credit control problems.

Design and Production Process

Every month a production list is prepared from which Jan works, and at the start of each month she knows exactly how many of each doll need to be produced. In a limited edition, each dealer is allocated dolls and numbers. Most dealers and collectors prefer the lower numbers of the limited edition models.

Each doll is designed by Jan, including all of the many different clothes and accessories that are included. Inspiration for her doll design comes from personal experiences of everyday life. Some dolls are modeled on her daughter, Kimberlee; others have input from pictures seen in magazines and books. The designs are then discussed with the dressmaker, who calculates the sizing for the clothes, and the two mold makers, who, with a great deal of patience and skill, make the molds out of clay. It is possible to get 50–60 casings from a mold before it wears out. Once the production run is finished, the molds are destroyed to preserve the limited-edition nature of the dolls.

Production of dolls in the factory requires some plant and machinery. There is a mixer for the porcelain clay, four electric kilns for firing the doll components in their molds, two electric mould driers, an air compressor, two extraction fans for taking out the dust and fumes and three sewing machines and an overlocker for making clothes and accessories.

The production process starts with liquid porcelain clay imported from America in small plastic tubs. This is an expensive raw material, but no better alternative supply has been found. The quality of clay available in New Zealand is not good enough to produce the fine porcelain clay finish required for dolls' faces, arms and legs. The clay is mixed, poured into molds, and left to set. The body parts are then dried, sanded and kiln-fired, where they shrink in size by about 20 percent. The parts are then re-sanded, oiled, and hand painted. Material costs are less than 15 percent of total production costs.

At this stage Jan, who is solely responsible for all dolls' faces, painstakingly hand paints the face details, firing the heads in the kiln several times as different details are added to the face. The dolls eyes are placed and fixed in the head, which is then complete. Other body parts, hands, and legs are made in the factory and inspected. During the production process, quality is inspected at every stage.

When all body parts and heads are ready, they are sent to an outworker who assembles the dolls' bodies. Bodies, costumes, accessories, and wigs are then stockpiled, ready for assembly. Jan believes that the design of the dolls makes them attractive as well as the high visual quality of every part.

When an order is scheduled, the head is put onto the body and a wig is added. Each doll is usually put onto a stand and then it is ready for the final quality check. Two workers inspect all parts of the finished dolls using a checklist of quality features. One copy of this checklist is sent with the doll to the customer while another copy is filed for reference. The quality of the face is the most important feature; a hairline crack on the face can diminish the value of the doll substantially.

Packaging for each doll for courier post has been a major problem. There is no standard box available in New Zealand that is the right size for the dolls, so a custom-made box had been designed. One or two dolls can fit in these new boxes. At a cost of NZ$180–$200 per box, a doll once finished can be delivered by courier anywhere in the world within four days.

Jan has bought the premises adjoining the factory, where she plans to move the dusty production processes (such as sanding) once the current lease expires. This will help to further enhance the working conditions and the quality of the dolls.

Personal Attributes

Jan believes in setting targets for herself and her staff. Usually these are production targets for the week. She has an overall objective to have an annual sales revenue of NZ$1 million. Along with this motivation, Jan also enjoys being her own boss, which allows her the opportunity to travel and to have a sense of achievement from her accomplishments.

A typical day for Jan can be characterized by her comment, "there doesn't seem to be enough hours in most days." Because she needs to attend annual toy fairs such as the one in New York, she must stockpile enough hand-painted components for the factory operations to continue in her absence, since she is the only person who can paint the faces and check the finished quality. Jan delegates many administrative matters to others to allow her to perform the many duties she has in the factory, which range from public relations to material purchasing to doll designing. Typically, she is able to leave the factory at about 6 P.M. each evening, although when orders need to be completed, extra working time is often required of Jan and her staff.

When asked about the personal attributes that have helped her succeed in the business, Jan admits that she is hard working, diligent, a capable administrator and delegator, versatile and has good interpersonal skills. Her long experience in nursing probably contributes to her interpersonal skills and the strong rapport she develops with customers, suppliers, and employees. She has a passion for her work and will tell you that she also needed some luck. Even though collectors are willing to pay high prices for her dolls, Jan isn't satisfied.

> I want to be better. I know all the faults of my work and I want to be really good. I can't believe my good fortune and I pinch myself all the time. What did I do to deserve this? We have really created a monster! I never actually expected the success or the work involved in performing this sort of operation. It's immensely demanding, the time and effort required is quite phenomenal, and I must say, I'm not used to having a high public profile; however, the personal rewards are extremely satisfying for both myself and my family.

Jan is also able to draw on the talents of those other than the on-site employees in the day-to-day running of the business. Her public accountant acts as a financial advisor when required, and their business relationship has been good. He monitors the cash flow and provides financial management, but the business has almost always run on cash generated with the occasional use of overdraft facilities. Jan foresees him taking a more active role in the future. Her husband, who is employed by the Inland Revenue Department, is able to take charge of all taxation matters, while one of her sons, who is an electrician, helps with any building and machinery maintenance problems.

Jan's daughter, Kimberlee, works in the factory where she loads the kilns, sands and paints the limbs and heads, makes and styles the wigs and assists in the dressing of the dolls, while another son, Hayden, assists in the making and pouring of the molds. Jan, however, is adamant that when she isn't at the factory, rather than leave one of her children in charge, the employees act as a team to solve any problems that arise. There is also a secretary working at the factory who handles all dispatch documents, typing, helping with stock ordering and general inquiries and deals with the American agents and customers.

Leoni, the dressmaker, keeps track of all fabric and lace stock levels and reorders when necessary. There is no formal stock control system. Jan always has a rough idea of the material stock levels. She frequently buys material on impulse when she knows it will look great at a later date when required.

Jan has experienced a number of problems during her doll making career. She found that, as a woman, she was not privy to the established "old boys" network. Several businessmen, including her bank manager, did not take her business plans seriously until she had proved her business was successful. In practice, this meant that she was sometimes excluded from information networks which might have been useful, and it was sometimes frustrating having to regularly prove her credibility as a businessperson before she was given access to required information or contacts. She has also found that her managerial skills have been on a learning curve since entering the doll making profession, but she has learned to overcome many problems and adapt to different situations as they arise.

Obtaining materials has been another problem. A number of the materials she uses are not available in New Zealand, which frustrates her, as she is forced to find materials overseas. For example, she imports mohair fabric from England, and baby carriages and other accessories from Indonesia. The porcelain clay mix and some accessories come from America. This has led to a number of associated problems. Most materials must be stockpiled to have them on hand when needed. Purchasing just when required is an attractive option; however, it seems impossible at this stage. This results in large levels of capital tied up in stock. If Jan is working on a limited edition line, she must ensure that there is enough material on hand for the entire line. Even though the line may not be produced all at once, Jan is required to buy in bulk in order to have the materials in stock when required.

There have also been difficulties in the past when key staff have left the company. This has been counteracted by taking the positive step of making sure that everyone employed can also perform another person's task. If time allowed, every person could be trained to carry out every part of the production process except for face and hand painting. Job rotation and job sharing have also been introduced. Now, if one of the employees is sick, someone can take over more easily.

At this stage, Jan's design and painting skills are the only ones that cannot be replaced easily. Teaching these skills to anyone else is difficult and time consuming. Jan intends to train her daughter to assist her. However, training family members has problems, particularly with young adults not wanting to be tied down.

Another problem Jan faces is that she is not able to get ahead of demand and stockpile finished dolls. Stockpiling would be an attractive option because it would reduce customer waiting time considerably. Components, materials, and accessories are stocked, but the hand-painting of the faces and checking the finished doll create the bottleneck in the production process.

So, where to now for Jan McLean Originals? Jan is highly aware that doll collecting could quite easily go out of fashion, and she is, therefore, conscious of the need to make a decision on the direction that Jan McLean Originals should take in the future. She has seriously considered mass producing lower-priced dolls with her brand name. This would probably lower the desirability of her limited-edition dolls. If mass production was licensed to a larger company, the royalties could be substantial enough for Jan to live very comfortably, or she could pursue another career change. If her dolls are mass produced, Jan is adamant that this should be done in New Zealand rather than in Asia where the finished quality of the products would be lower. Although production costs would also be lower, Jan does not want to compromise her reputation for high quality.

Another option would be to expand operations in the factory and possibly diversify into other products, for example, collectible teddy bears. She is not over-confident about managing a larger operation herself, because her time spent painting doll faces is precious and she does not have the confidence in her managerial abilities to run a larger factory successfully. A large expansion would require a new factory manager and other staff.

Questions

1. Are Jan McLean Originals an appropriate product for direct marketing? Discuss the characteristics of the doll in relation to successful direct marketing products.
2. Assuming the current doll could be sold successfully by mail, what would be the characteristics of a successful list? What are some of the elements that would likely be in a successful McLean Originals' offer? A successful positioning? A successful medium/format?
3. Assuming Jan McLean decided to mass produce a lower-quality doll, would this change the following:
    a. Its chance for success in the direct mail channel?
    b. Its needed list characteristics?
    c. Its needed offer characteristics?
    d. Its needed program structure?
    e. Its format characteristics?
4. What would be Jan McLean's fulfillment concerns if she launched into a big direct marketing program, given current products and production? Given a move to mass production of a lower-quality doll? Given a move to aggressive direct marketing in other countries?

This case was prepared by T.W. Batley and D.J. Tapp, University of Otago, New Zealand. At the time of writing (1994), the NZ/US exchange rate was NZ$1.00= US$0.60.

TITLES OF INTEREST IN MARKETING, DIRECT MARKETING, AND SALES PROMOTION

SUCCESSFUL DIRECT MARKETING METHODS, by Bob Stone
PROFITABLE DIRECT MARKETING, by Jim Kobs
INTEGRATED DIRECT MARKETING, by Ernan Roman
BEYOND 2000: THE FUTURE OF DIRECT MARKETING, by Jerry I. Reitman
POWER DIRECT MARKETING, by "Rocket" Ray Jutkins
CREATIVE STRATEGY IN DIRECT MARKETING, by Susan K. Jones
SECRETS OF SUCCESSFUL DIRECT MAIL, by Richard V. Benson
STRATEGIC DATABASE MARKETING, by Rob Jackson and Paul Wang
SUCCESSFUL TELEMARKETING, by Bob Stone and John Wyman
BUSINESS TO BUSINESS DIRECT MARKETING, by Robert Bly
COMMONSENSE DIRECT MARKETING, by Drayton Bird
DIRECT MARKETING CHECKLISTS, by John Stockwell and Henry Shaw
INTEGRATED MARKETING COMMUNICATIONS, by Don E. Schultz, Stanley I. Tannenbaum, and Robert F. Lauterborn
NEW DIRECTIONS IN MARKETING, by Aubrey Wilson
GREEN MARKETING, by Jacquelyn Ottman
MARKETING CORPORATE IMAGE: THE COMPANY AS YOUR NUMBER ONE PRODUCT, by James R. Gregory with Jack G. Wiechmann
HOW TO CREATE SUCCESSFUL CATALOGS, by Maxwell Sroge
101 TIPS FOR MORE PROFITABLE CATALOGS, by Maxwell Sroge
SALES PROMOTION ESSENTIALS, by Don E. Schultz, William A. Robinson and Lisa A. Petrison
PROMOTIONAL MARKETING, by William A. Robinson and Christine Hauri
BEST SALES PROMOTIONS, by William A. Robinson
INSIDE THE LEADING MAIL ORDER HOUSES, by Maxwell Sroge
NEW PRODUCT DEVELOPMENT, by George Gruenwald
NEW PRODUCT DEVELOPMENT CHECKLISTS, by George Gruenwald
CLASSIC FAILURES IN PRODUCT MARKETING, by Donald W. Hendon
HOW TO TURN CUSTOMER SERVICE INTO CUSTOMER SALES, by Bernard Katz
ADVERTISING & MARKETING CHECKLISTS, by Ron Kaatz
BRAND MARKETING, by William M. Weilbacher
MARKETING WITHOUT MONEY, by Nicholas E. Bade
THE 1-DAY MARKETING PLAN, by Roman A. Hiebing, Jr. and Scott W. Cooper
HOW TO WRITE A SUCCESSFUL MARKETING PLAN, by Roman G. Hiebing, Jr. and Scott W. Cooper
DEVELOPING, IMPLEMENTING, AND MANAGING EFFECTIVE MARKETING PLANS, by Hal Goetsch
HOW TO EVALUATE AND IMPROVE YOUR MARKETING DEPARTMENT, by Keith Sparling and Gerard Earls
SELLING TO A SEGMENTED MARKET, by Chester A. Swenson
MARKET-ORIENTED PRICING, by Michael Morris and Gene Morris
STATE-OF-THE-ART MARKETING RESEARCH, by A.B. Blankenship and George E. Breen
AMA HANDBOOK FOR CUSTOMER SATISFACTION, by Alan Dutka
WAS THERE A PEPSI GENERATION BEFORE PEPSI DISCOVERED IT?, by Stanley C. Hollander and Richard Germain
BUSINESS TO BUSINESS COMMUNICATIONS HANDBOOK, by Fred Messner
MANAGING SALES LEADS: HOW TO TURN EVERY PROSPECT INTO A CUSTOMER, by Robert Donath, Richard Crocker, Carol Dixon and James Obermeyer
AMA MARKETING TOOLBOX (SERIES), by David Parmerlee
AMA COMPLETE GUIDE TO SMALL BUSINESS MARKETING, by Kenneth J. Cook
AMA COMPLETE GUIDE TO STRATEGIC PLANNING FOR SMALL BUSINESS, by Kenneth J. Cook
AMA COMPLETE GUIDE TO SMALL BUSINESS ADVERTISING, by Joe Vitale
HOW TO GET THE MOST OUT OF TRADE SHOWS, by Steve Miller
HOW TO GET THE MOST OUT OF SALES MEETINGS, by James Dance
STRATEGIC MARKET PLANNING, by Robert J. Hamper and L. Sue Baugh

For further information or a current catalog, write:
NTC Business Books
a division of NTC Publishing Group
4255 West Touhy Avenue
Lincolnwood, Illinois 60646–1975 U.S.A.